I0802669

·EX·LIBRIS·

“

This book is packed with wanderlust fuel for the adventurous book addict.

MR. B’S EMPORIUM OF READING DELIGHTS, BATH

A World of Bookish Places *is an atlas of wonder and a testament to the endless places your curiosity can take you.*

STRAND BOOKSTORE, NEW YORK CITY

What a joy to have this collection of wonderful literary landmarks and community spaces. You’re sure to find books to add to your to-be-read list and places to add to your to-be-visited.

ELLIOTT BAY BOOK COMPANY, SEATTLE

A World of Bookish Places *is a glorious ode to book lovers and bookshops alike; whether it’s used as a bucket list or for bookshelf inspiration, this is a guide not to be missed.*

TOPPING & COMPANY BOOKSELLERS, BATH

DK

A World *of* Bookish Places

Travel inspiration for book lovers

Introduction 6

New York City 10

Boston 18

Chicago 26

Washington, D.C. 30

New Orleans 34

Seattle 40

San Francisco 44

Vancouver 52

Mexico City 58

Bogotá 64

Rio de Janeiro 70

Buenos Aires 74

London 80

Oxford 88

Bath 94

Edinburgh 100

Dublin 106

Paris 110

Madrid 118

Lisbon 124

Florence 128

Vienna 134

Berlin 140

Leipzig 146

Weimar 150

Copenhagen 154

Prague 162

Istanbul 168

Cairo 174

Shanghai 180

Seoul 184

Tokyo 190

Bangkok 198

Melbourne 204

Wellington 210

More Bookish Places 214

Index 218

Acknowledgments 222

Shakespeare and Company, Paris

Introduction

All book lovers know that feeling: you're a few pages into a novel and suddenly find yourself whisked away to another world—a new city, a far-off country, or even an entirely fantastical realm. That's the joy and magic of a good book. It doesn't just tell a story, it transports you.

But while we might love traveling *through* books, what about traveling *for* books? If you're anything like us, the first thing you seek out in a new city isn't a landmark but a bookstore tucked down a quiet street, a grand old library, or a café where a writer once sat and penned a novel. The world's great cities are shaped not only by people and events, but by the stories they've inspired—and today, they remain full of places that cherish the written word.

We editors count ourselves incredibly lucky. Working here at DK Travel, we get to bring together our two greatest pleasures—books and travel—every single day. And when we're not at our desks, you'll likely find us wandering the aisles of a bookstore or plotting our next literary pilgrimage. A weekend in Paris wouldn't feel complete without an hour spent in Shakespeare and Company, just as a trip to New York calls for a visit to the New York Public Library. For us, these places are as essential as any museum or monument.

Working on *A World of Bookish Places* has been a true joy, though not without its challenges. First came the impossible task of choosing just 35 literary cities (spoiler: we couldn't quite manage it, which is why you'll find an additional 24 bookish places on pages 214–217).

Then came the even harder part: narrowing down the countless bookstores, libraries, and literary landmarks within those cities. Needless to say there are a near-infinite number of bookstores and other literary landmarks that we—and the magicians who wielded their magic in writing this book—wanted to celebrate. But there are only so many pages …

This book is, at its heart, a love letter to the spaces that house the written word. In a world where life is becoming more digital, physical tomes and the places that treasure them are all the more important. There's something quietly sacred about browsing the stacks in a library and swapping recommendations with a bookseller, just as there is in holding a crisp new book in your hands.

The cities and bookish places within these pages have been treasured by fellow book lovers for generations. We hope they will continue to inspire many more journeys—both across the page and around the world—for years to come.

The Editors

Bookish Places

To enter *A World of Bookish Places*, you'll first need a key …

We've divided the literary landmarks in this book into the following groups.

BOOKSTORES

LIBRARIES

MUSEUMS & CREATIVE SPACES

LITERARY BARS & CAFÉS

BOOK MARKETS & STREETS

CEMETERIES & MONUMENTS

Cuesta de Moyano, Madrid

New York Public Library

New York City

NEW YORK, US | NORTH AMERICA

Home to beloved authors, renowned bookstores and epic libraries—and the setting for some of the world's most-read novels—this East Coast icon is easily America's most bookish city.

The Age of Innocence. The Great Gatsby. A Little Life. It's safe to say that most people have read a book set in New York. The Big Apple has appeared in some 80,000 novels, but it's rarely a static backdrop. Sometimes it's elegant and romantic—a city of dreamers, theater-lovers, and the arty upper class—yet in other stories it can be gritty and chaotic—all honking car horns, busy nine-to-fivers, and loud dive bars. New York has many faces; it depends on the book and the author as to which one you see.

For years, storytellers have fallen in love with the City that Never Sleeps. In the 19th century, Walt Whitman transformed his "city of spires and masts" into poetry. In the 20th century, the Harlem Renaissance saw African American music and literature flourish here. And around the same time, the Algonquin Round Table group—including cofounder of *The New Yorker* Harold Ross and critic Dorothy Parker—met to discuss their work.

The city remains a hub of creativity today, bursting with plays, poetry readings, spoken-word events—you name it. As for its literary history, well, that's pounded into the pavement, performed on Broadway, and proudly displayed in bookstores. New York's story is still being written, but it has plenty to tell you in the meantime.

GETTING AROUND

Most New Yorkers walk or take the subway—it's easier to navigate than it looks. Hail a cab if you want to pretend you're in a movie (and don't mind the traffic).

READING LIST

The Catcher in the Rye

J. D. Salinger

A classic coming-of-age story set among the city's landmarks, exploring the disillusionment of teenagehood through protagonist Holden Caulfield.

A Tree Grows in Brooklyn

Betty Smith

Examining the immigrant experience in Brooklyn, this beloved classic follows resilient Francie Nolan as she grows up in early-20th-century America.

The Goldfinch

Donna Tartt

After losing his mother in a terrorist attack at New York's Metropolitan Museum of Art, Theo Decker steals a painting, leading him into the darkest corners of the art world, and an obsession that defines his adulthood.

Strand Bookstore

From the 1890s until the 1960s, the area around Union Square (near the Flatiron Building) was home to more than 40 used bookstores and was known as "Book Row." Today, only one remains: Strand Bookstore. Claiming "18 miles of books"—four stories of new and used titles—this is the largest independent bookstore in the city, and it's become quite the cultural icon. Countless films and TV shows have been shot here, numerous famous folk have worked behind the register (including musician Patti Smith) and its logo totes are veritable status symbols. But for most New Yorkers, it's simply a great local bookstore. Join them dashing in to pick up a last-minute gift, hunting down an out-of-print title, or sheltering under the red awning when the rain rolls in.

☞ 828 Broadway, Union Square; strandbooks.com

Strand Bookstore

White Horse Tavern

"Do not go gentle into that good night," wrote poet Dylan Thomas—and when he wanted to have a good night, he'd go to the White Horse Tavern, one of New York's oldest bars. This British-inspired pub began as a humble hangout for dock workers, before it was transformed into a writers' haunt in the 1950s; besides the Welsh poet, regulars included American writers James Baldwin and Norman Mailer. Legend has it that Thomas drank 18 whiskeys here before collapsing into a fatal coma outside ("rage, rage" indeed). While a bit of moderation might not go amiss, you can still drink in the footsteps of great authors at the tavern's worn wooden bar or in a tufted leather booth, book and burger in hand.

☞ 567 Hudson Street, West Village; whitehorsetavern1880.com

Poets House

Poets House is, as you'd expect, a place for all things poetry—reading, writing, learning, and sharing. A nonprofit founded in 1985 by poet Stanley Kunitz and housed in a glass-fronted building, it overlooks the Hudson River and offers a quiet retreat from the hustle and bustle of the city (it's free and open to the public five days a week). Sunlight filters through the large windows in the airy library, which contains 80,000 books of English-language poetry. Special collections include audio recordings from American masters like ee cummings and Sylvia Plath, chapbooks and rare first editions. But Poets House doesn't just memorialize the past; it's on a mission to amplify the voices of modern bards through workshops, youth programs and showcases that highlight up-and-coming artists and diverse cultural perspectives.

☞ 10 River Terrace, Battery Park City; poetshouse.org

Morgan Library and Museum

Morgan Library and Museum

In 1906, investment banker J. P. Morgan commissioned a library fit for a king: picture elaborate painted ceilings, lush studies full of Renaissance artwork and floor-to-ceiling walnut bookshelves. Luckily for New Yorkers, it didn't stay private forever—Morgan's son donated the repository to the public in 1924. Inside, you'll find exquisite manuscripts, handwritten materials, and early drafts from greats like Mozart and Michelangelo. Naturally, academics flock here for scholarly residencies—but you don't need a degree to be wowed by all this beauty.

225 Madison Avenue, Midtown; themorgan.org

New York Public Library

The Beaux-Arts branch of the New York Public Library is *enormous*. Lofty columns and stately lion statues mark its entrance, and inside there are more than 2.5 million volumes, plus a reading room spanning two city blocks. It's the second-largest library in the US (the largest is in Washington, D.C., p.32), and while you could spend hours wandering its halls, you'll find hunting down its bizarre literary artifacts even more exciting. Look for a lock of Charlotte Brontë's hair, a paper knife adorned with the foot of Charles Dickens' cat (yes, a real foot!), original Winnie the Pooh dolls, and a Gutenberg Bible.

476 5th Avenue, Midtown; nypl.org

The Drama Book Shop

The Drama Book Shop

If all the world's a stage, New York stands front and center as the musical theater capital of the globe. And when performers arrive to cut their teeth on Broadway, they head to the Drama Book Shop. Stocking more than 8,000 plays and a recipient of the Tony Honor for Excellence in Theatre, this bookshop is every theater kid's dream. After 100 years in business, the shop was under threat of closure until Lin-Manuel Miranda, of *Hamilton* fame, stepped in to save it in 2019. Its new digs were outfitted by set designer David Korins and are, quite rightly, show-stopping. A swirling sculpture of books winds through the rafters, warm wood shelves house stacks of scripts, and the smell of coffee wafts from the café, creating the perfect setting for some "table reading."

266 W 39th Street, Midtown; dramabookshop.com

Argosy

The oldest independent bookstore in New York City, Argosy feels like stepping into the pages of a rare book: beautiful, special, and a world unto itself. Occupying a six-story townhouse around the corner from Bloomingdale's, its open-air, book-filled lobby beckons you in from the street. Inside, a vintage elevator transports you between floors, while warm wooden shelves show off the shop's many treasures, from rare maps of Manhattan to old leather book covers and autographed collectors' items. This specialized collective has lured in many noteworthy customers over the years—President Franklin D. Roosevelt, composer Stephen Sondheim, and designer Donatella Versace, to name a few—but this isn't just a place for the highbrow. The family-owned gem also stocks cheap paperbacks and hosts an annual "basement sale," where the entire floor is marked 50 percent off.

116 E 59th Street, Midtown; argosybooks.com

Albertine

Albertine

There's a certain *je ne sais quoi* to Albertine, a French bookstore housed inside a Gilded Age mansion on the Upper East Side. Stepping into the Italian Renaissance–style building is an experience in itself—think marble rotundas and ornate fireplaces—but the true magic is tucked behind a nondescript double doorway. Beyond is the shop's reading room, a depiction of the zodiac swirling across a celestial ceiling, painted in indigo and gold. Moody lanterns illuminate leather sofas and cozy nooks, where Francophiles flip through French and English titles from more than 30 French-speaking countries. A project of the French Embassy, Albertine's mission is to facilitate intellectual exchange and friendship across cultures—not just through reading, but also through lectures, debates, and discussions.

☞ 972 5th Avenue, Upper East Side; albertine.com

Edgar Allan Poe Cottage

On a busy highway in the Bronx, Edgar Allan Poe's cottage sticks out like a sore thumb, a modest white farmhouse nearly eclipsed by modern architecture and ever-rising high-rise apartments. The American poet moved to the home in 1849 to escape the city, hoping the then-pastoral setting would heal his ailing wife, Virginia. Poe spent his final days here, writing works like "Annabel Lee" and "Ulalume"—reflections on love and loss that mirror the experiences he had while residing in the house. Today, the five-room cottage is open for tours and furnished to show what it might have looked like when Poe lived here—a time when the Bronx was filled with picket fences and apple orchards, a version of the city that will be nevermore.

☞ 2640 Grand Concourse, The Bronx; bronxhistoricalsociety.org/poe-cottage

BOOK AT BEDTIME

Hotel Chelsea

Creative folk have long flocked to the Hotel Chelsea. Splash out on one of the decadent rooms in this Chelsea-based artistic haven and you'll be in the company of innumerable greats, including Jack Kerouac, Janis Joplin, and Jimi Hendrix *(hotelchelsea.com)*.

Harlem Renaissance

During the 1920s, the New York neighborhood of Harlem became a hotbed of African American creativity. The Harlem Renaissance, as it became known, saw artists, poets, and musicians gather in local jazz clubs and homes here to rewrite what it meant to be a Black American.

DISTANCE
2 miles (3 km)

WALKING TIME
Allow an hour

NEAREST TRANSIT
Harlem–125th Street station is near the start of the route; 135th Street is near the end

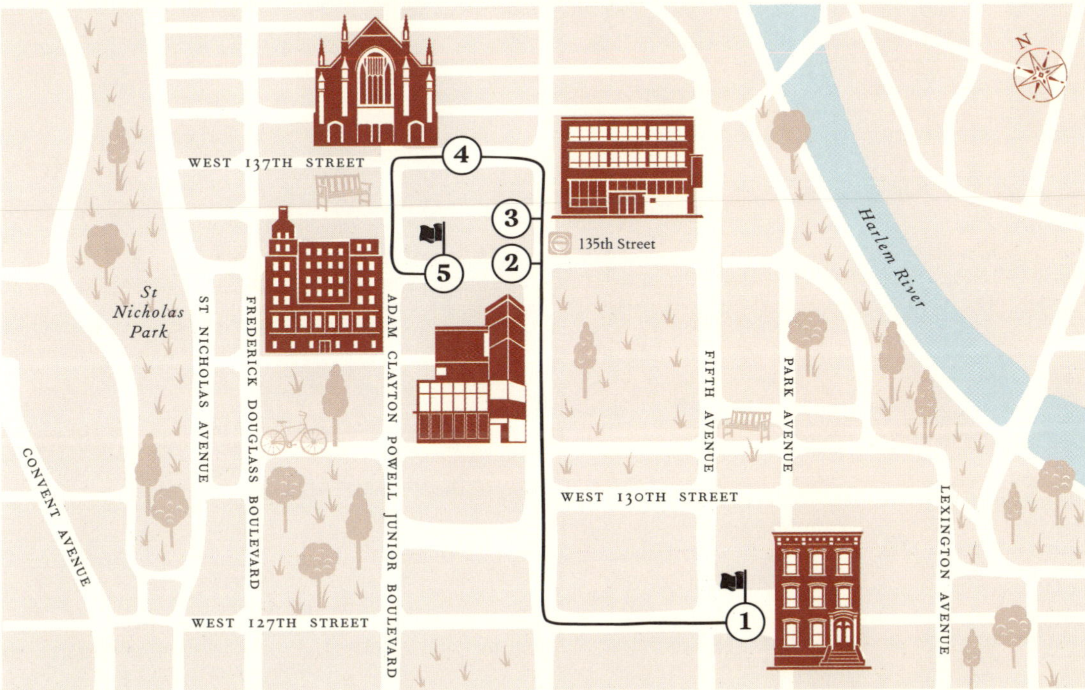

1. Langston Hughes House

This ivy-covered brownstone was once the home of renowned poet Langston Hughes, a key figure in the Harlem Renaissance. It's now a house-museum dedicated to him *(20 E 127th St.)*.

2. Schomburg Center

This repository of Black culture was formed using historian and writer Arturo Schomburg's collection of books and art. It's also home to Langston Hughes's ashes *(515 Malcolm X Blvd)*.

3. Countee Cullen Library

The eponymous poet used to frequent the original branch of this library. Its new premises are on the site of heiress A'Lelia Walker's house, where she hosted lavish Harlem parties *(104 W 136th St.)*.

4. Mother AME Zion Church

Dating to 1796, this church counted Black writers such as W. E. B. Du Bois and Langston Hughes among its congregation. It was later a gathering place for civil rights activists *(140 W 137th St.)*.

5. Harlem YMCA

In the 1920s, many of the Renaissance's literati lived and worked in the Harlem YMCA, among them beloved poet Claude McKay. Today, the building is a youth center *(180 W 135th St.)*.

Brattle Book Shop

Boston

MASSACHUSETTS, US | NORTH AMERICA

Sometimes called "the Athens of America," Boston has long been an intellectual center of the US. It's the birthplace of American independence and American literature, where revolutionary ideas and talented writers shaped the voice of a fledgling nation.

When it comes to US cities, they don't get more historic than Boston. Founded in 1630, the colonial capital is considered the birthplace of the American Revolution, and it was here that the Founding Fathers introduced democratic ideals that would come to change the course of history.

But Boston wasn't just revolutionary for its politics. In the 1800s, the city became the epicenter of the country's literary output. It was here that American Romanticism—a style that celebrated national landscapes and the spirit of individualism—took shape under the pen of writers like Nathaniel Hawthorne. Transcendentalism *(p.25)* was also dreamed up in the city's taverns, by spiritual nature lovers Ralph Waldo Emerson and Henry David Thoreau. Diverging from European traditions, these writers laid the groundwork for American literature as we know it today.

You can still trace their footsteps, spotting author homes down cobblestone streets or discovering their work in thriving indie bookstores. And if you start to question whether Boston is still setting the tone of American literature, just head to Harvard. The first university in the US remains a hub of creativity, nurturing the free-thinking writers of tomorrow.

GETTING AROUND

Boston's public transit system, the "T," was revolutionary, too: it's the first subway system in the US. The city is also fairly walkable; follow the Freedom Trail for a self-guided tour of its most historic sites.

READING LIST

The Bostonians

Henry James

First published as a serial in a magazine, this satirical tragi-comedy recounts the struggle between a Southern conservative and a Northern feminist for the attention of a young woman.

The Living Is Easy

Dorothy West

Dorothy West's acclaimed novel follows ambitious antihero Cleo Judson as she navigates life in Boston's Black upper-middle-class community.

Mystic River

Dennis Lehane

This gripping psychological thriller tells the story of three childhood friends in Boston who are brought together again in adulthood following a traumatic event. A film adaptation was released in 2003.

Boston Athenaeum

Founded in 1807, the Boston Athenaeum was envisioned as a place for members and guests to study, work, and gather—an early version of today's coworking hubs, perhaps. Now, as one of the oldest independent libraries in the country, it houses some 100,000 works of art and half a million books, including a number of rare treasures. Over the years, writers like Louisa May Alcott and Nathaniel Hawthorne have found solace inside its hallowed halls, while today's members can enjoy stunning 19th-century architecture, literary discussion groups, and on-site dining. The cultural center might bring all of life's finer things together under one roof, but like Boston, it's surprisingly democratic—the nonprofit offers affordable single-day memberships.

☞ 10-1/2 Beacon Street, Beacon Hill; bostonathenaeum.org

Omni Parker House

In 1855, a circle of authors and intellectuals began gathering monthly at the Parker House for dinner and discussions about literature, art, and science. This informal salon, led by Ralph Waldo Emerson, Henry Wadsworth Longfellow, and Oliver Wendell Holmes Sr., to name a few, eventually became the legendary Saturday Club—an invitation-only organization that marked one's entrance into Boston's creative high society. Today, the Parker House is the nation's longest-operating hotel and, despite modern updates by the Omni hotel group, maintains many ties to its storied past. Try the original Boston cream pie—a chocolaty concoction invented in the on-site restaurant—or request a room on the third floor, reportedly haunted by Charles Dickens. The author's ghost has also, apparently, appeared in the mirror where he rehearsed readings of *A Christmas Carol* during his stay. The mirror is now located in a corridor on the hotel's mezzanine, and some say if you chant "Charles Dickens" three times in front of it, the nearby elevator bells will chime ....

☞ 60 School Street, Downtown; omnihotels.com

Brattle Book Shop

One of the oldest and largest used book sellers in the US, Brattle Book Shop blends the elegance of an antique bookstore with the charm of a beloved flea market. The rummaging begins outdoors in a brick courtyard, where overflowing carts evoke a street fair and shelves carry novels priced at $1, $3, and $5. Inside the 200-year-old outpost, you'll find more than 250,000 used books, maps, and postcards, plus a third floor dedicated to out-of-print collectibles and first editions (it doesn't hurt that the owner appraises books for the likes of Boston College and the FBI). On your way out, arms full of treasures, pause for a photo beneath the giant pencil above the entryway—it's an obligatory photo shoot for book lovers who come to the city.

☞ 9 West Street, Downtown; brattlebookshop.com

LITERARY FESTIVAL

Boston Book Festival

Live music, food trucks, author talks, creative workshops: the Boston Book Festival always promises a good time for book lovers. It takes place every year (generally in October) in venues like the Boston Public Library. Best of all, most events are free.

Beacon Hill Books & Café

Tucked inside a five-story townhouse steps away from the Charles River, Beacon Hill Books & Café feels straight out of a Regency romance. Head up the stairs and through the red doorway and you'll discover cozy reading nooks, crackling fireplaces, and colorful parlor seating that all invite you to stay awhile. Whimsical touches abound, from a toy train circling the ceiling to the shop's fictional squirrel, Paige—she's featured in decor, gifts, and her very own children's book. After browsing a curated selection of New England literature and other titles, duck through a hobbit-sized back doorway to the shop's elevated all-day café and garden, perfect for an afternoon soiree. The thinkers of yesteryear may have met at the Parker House, but the creatives of today gather here.

71 Charles Street, Beacon Hill; bhbooks.com

Harvard Book Store

Harvard Book Store

There are universities, and then there is Harvard. Founded in 1636 as the first college in the US and consistently ranked among the nation's most rigorous schools, Harvard has many an author among its distinguished alumni, from T. S. Eliot to Henry James. It's hardly a surprise, then, that the indie bookstore that shares its name is also one of the best in class—an intellectual hub and cultural institution serving the Cambridge community since 1932. The family-owned shop is particularly beloved for its seasonal warehouse sales and award-winning author events featuring Pulitzer Prize winners and university lecturers. Spend an afternoon browsing its academic titles or used book basement, and you can honestly claim you "went to Harvard"—no one has to know which one.

1256 Massachusetts Avenue, Cambridge; harvard.com

Frugal Bookstore

With the motto "Changing minds one book at a time," it's clear that Frugal Bookstore is on a mission—not just to keep printed books alive, but to promote literacy and cultural pride in the Roxbury neighborhood. The city's only Black-owned bookstore, Frugal spotlights authors of color, reflecting the identity and soul of the community it serves. Titles include antiracist literature and children's books, plus a variety of fiction featuring diverse characters. Recently recognized as a legacy business for its longstanding contributions to the city, this place is an icon of Boston's literary scene.

57 Warren Street, Roxbury; frugalbookstore.net

Boston Public Library

Libraries today are known for being free and open to all, but this wasn't always the case. For centuries, they housed the private collections of the wealthy or acted as members-only organizations renting books on subscription. In the 19th century, that began to change, and Boston, as usual, was at the forefront. The city launched the first public library in the US, which was the first to loan out books to everyday folks. But don't let its proletarian roots fool you—the 1895 Renaissance Revival building is a stunner, designed as a palace for the people. Halls feature floor-to-ceiling marble walls and an abundance of paintings, while the reading room could double as an Italian cathedral. You can even book your own "Boston tea party" at the library, with afternoon tea served in the courtyard Wednesday to Sunday.

☞ 700 Boylston Street, Back Bay; bpl.org

Forest Hills Cemetery

An unexpectedly beautiful place to spend an afternoon, Forest Hills Cemetery isn't just the final resting place of notable authors like abolitionist William Lloyd Garrison and poet ee cummings; it's also an open-air museum, arboretum, and public park listed on the National Register of Historic Places. Across its leafy sprawl, trails wind beneath flowering trees and among sculptures and fascinating grave markers, from tender statues of departed children to sprawling Victorian mausoleums. Hidden treasures await at every turn—you might spot the grave of Lewis Edson Waterman, the inventor of the fountain pen, or a miniature model of poet Anne Sexton's home. Here in this serene setting, the spirit of the Transcendentalists lingers, inviting you to connect with nature and contemplate what lies beyond.

☞ 95 Forest Hills Avenue, Jamaica Plain; foresthillscemetery.com

Boston Public Library

Orchard House

Concord

MASSACHUSETTS, US | NORTH AMERICA

Shaded by pine and maple trees, little Concord has had an outsize impact on American history. In 1775, it played host to the opening battle of the American Revolution; roughly 60 years later, it became a fulcrum of literary brilliance. The latter was thanks to four authors—Ralph Waldo Emerson, Henry David Thoreau, Louisa May Alcott, and Nathaniel Hawthorne—who wrote some of the most influential works of the era here.

Ralph Waldo Emerson House

Emerson spent over 50 years in this house, where he held regular gatherings of the town's intellectuals. It's still owned by the family and contains original furniture and personal effects.

rwema.org/visit-the-emerson-house

Thoreau's Cabin at Walden Pond

Thoreau's *Walden* was inspired by the two years he spent living in a cabin next to Walden Pond. The original cabin was removed, but you can still visit its location and admire a replica.

mass.gov/locations/walden-pond-state-reservation

Orchard House

The Alcott's family home is where Louisa May and her three sisters spent part of their childhood. It's also where she penned *Little Women*—you can see the desk she wrote at on a tour.

louisamayalcott.org

The Old Manse

Emerson wrote both *Nature* and *The Concord Hymn*, commemorating the first battle of the American Revolution, at his grandparents' house.

visitconcord.org

In 1834, Ralph Waldo Emerson came to Concord to live in his grandparents' house. Here, the quiet beauty of the scenery moved him to compose *Nature*, a now-iconic essay that helped birth Transcendentalism (a movement with a deep appreciation of the natural world). Over the following decades, Emerson—and Concord itself—inspired other writers who found their way here, among them Nathaniel Hawthorne, author of *The Scarlet Letter*, and fellow Transcendentalist Henry David Thoreau, of *Walden* fame. The trio met in Emerson's house for thought-provoking discussions and debates; joining them was Amos Alcott, father of Louisa May, whose beloved novel *Little Women* was inspired by her time here. Old clapboard homes belonging to these authors still stand today, as do Walden Pond, its "sky water," and surrounding woods.

Ralph Waldo Emerson

The Poetry Foundation

Chicago

ILLINOIS, US | NORTH AMERICA

New York might have the pedigree, Los Angeles the glamour, but Chicago is the heart of American letters. Writers here have made the record in their own way, creating not just sensational stories but trailblazing poetry, too.

"Find a writer who is indubitably an American in every pulse-beat, snort, and adenoid, an American who has something new and peculiarly American to say ... and nine times out of ten ... he has some sort of connection with [Chicago]." So said the great journalist H. L. Mencken, writing in *The Nation* magazine. That was 1920, and while Mencken likely had writers like Ida B. Wells *(The Red Record)* and L. Frank Baum *(The Wonderful Wizard of Oz)* in mind, his statement now seems as much prophecy as observation. In the years since, this city on the shores of Lake Michigan has given us titans like Saul Bellow, Ernest Hemingway, and Lorraine Hansberry, and writers who have shaped culture beyond literature, like movie critic Roger Ebert.

It's also been at the forefront of American poetry. The English-speaking world's oldest monthly journal of verse, *Poetry*, has been published here since 1912; icons like Carl Sandburg and Gwendolyn Brooks lived here; and the city's Green Mill Cocktail Lounge is considered the birthplace of slam poetry. Today, Chicago still champions verse as much as prose—artistic centers support new writers, and spoken-word events buzz as much as comedy clubs. In few American cities will you find a literary scene that feels so alive. The heart still beats.

GETTING AROUND

Chicago is a sprawling city of skyscrapers; to best get around, hop on the metro, commonly called the "L." For an alternative view of the city, take a river boat through the center.

READING LIST

Chicago Poems

Carl Sandburg

This influential poetry collection celebrates Chicago's raw energy and spirit; it's where the famous moniker "the City of Big Shoulders" came from.

The House on Mango Street

Sandra Cisneros

Told through a series of short vignettes, this novel follows a young girl growing up in Chicago's Hispanic neighborhoods, capturing the moments that shape her sense of identity and belonging.

Native Son

Richard Wright

Set in 1930s Chicago, this powerful novel examines race, poverty, and systemic injustice through the story of a young Black man whose life is irrevocably altered.

Pilsen Community Books

The best way to reach Pilsen Community Books (PCB) is to walk, taking time to explore Pilsen's vibrant Hispanic culture—tortillerias, Mexican restaurants, colorful murals—and hip boutiques, galleries, and music venues. The neighborhood is perfectly suited to PCB, Chicago's only employee-owned and -operated indie bookstore, whose vibe might best be described as confrontationally cozy. Classic bookstore features like wood floors and rolling library ladders share space with antifascist artwork and merch bearing the shop's slogan, "Always Carry a Book." And while PCB certainly isn't above stocking some classics, much of its inventory is devoted to leftist politics, shelved under categories like "Reproductive Justice," "Organizing," and "Labor." It also puts theory into practice through fundraisers, movie screenings, and a literacy program for young readers.

☞ 1531 W 18th Street, Pilsen; pilsencommunitybooks.com

American Writers Museum

Opened in 2017, this small downtown space is the country's only museum devoted to American authors. Exhibitions begin with a gallery of 100 writers who represent the evolution of American literature, from Álvar Núñez Cabeza de Vaca, the first European to record a detailed account of what's now the US, to the groundbreaking science fiction writer Philip K. Dick. The museum's purview goes well beyond author biographies, however, covering topics as diverse as Black newspapers, the history of book clubs, and the habits of prominent authors (poet Emily Dickinson baked award-winning cornmeal-and-rye bread). Interactive areas let you play games that take you inside the mind of a writer, and there are typewriters you can use to bang out a few lines.

☞ 180 N Michigan Avenue, 2nd Floor, The Loop; americanwritersmuseum.org

The Poetry Foundation

Chicago is a poetry town. And with a long legacy of verse writers and verse lovers, the "City of Big Shoulders" is also where you'll find the free-to-visit Poetry Foundation. This vital nonprofit supplies grants to upcoming poets, hosts various literary festivals, and now publishes the historic journal *Poetry*. The foundation's headquarters in the River North neighborhood also house the Midwest's only library dedicated to verse, with 40,000 volumes encompassing anthologies, chapbooks, and rare books—all housed in a gorgeous, light-filled gallery. In addition, the library features audio booths where visitors can listen to poetry recordings, read by their writers just as they were meant to be read. Inspired? Keep an eye out for the foundation's workshops.

☞ 61 W Superior Street, River North; poetryfoundation.org

Harold Washington Library Center

Even among Chicago's many eye-catching buildings, Harold Washington Library Center stands out. Opened as Chicago Public Library's central location in 1991, the red-brick structure occupies an entire city block and is crowned by a quintet of enormous owls. The largest, a 20-ft- (6-m-) tall great horned owl, perches above the main entrance. They guard some million literary items, alongside 50-plus acclaimed artwork displays throughout the building (pick up a guide in the lobby). There's also a fascinating exhibition devoted to the library's namesake, Chicago's first Black mayor and the man responsible for the library's construction. The exhibition is located on the ninth floor, along with a lovely winter garden (a conservatory-like space) where students read beneath the gleaming glassy roof. It's a stunning place, whether you're here for the books or not.

☞ 400 S State Street, The Loop; chipublib.org

The Joe and Rika Mansueto Library

Amid the University of Chicago's ivy-covered edifices, this campus library seems to bubble up from the future. Opened in 2011, it's enclosed within a yawning elliptical glass dome. Two-thirds of the library is devoted to the Grand Reading Room, where a studious hush pervades (grab a visitor's pass to enter); the rest houses a state-of-the-art book conservation lab. The most impressive part of the library, though, is what you can't see. When someone requests a book online, robotic cranes pluck the appropriate bin from 50-ft- (15-m-) tall subterranean stacks and send it to the surface, where a librarian removes the book and hands it over to the reader. The process takes just five minutes and requires only 14 percent as much space as conventional shelving.

☞ 1100 E 57th Street, Hyde Park; lib.uchicago.edu

The Joe and Rika Mansueto Library

Barnes & Noble

Is this Barnes & Noble's (B&N's) most beautiful bookstore? Stop by and you'll see for yourself. One of hundreds of B&N bookstores in America, the Wicker Park branch stands out from the crowd, largely thanks to its remarkable setting. It's housed in a grand old bank building, built in 1919 and thoughtfully restored before reopening as a bookstore in 2024. Many of the bank's original features remain, including the lofty entrance hall, gorgeous decorated ceiling, elegant hanging lights, and swoon-worthy stained-glass window—only now, book lovers wander where bankers once worked. Browsing the well-stocked shelves in such lovely surroundings is pure joy. Luckily for fans, there are plenty more B&N bookshops in the US (you'll find another favorite in Washington, D.C.; *p.32.*)

☞ 1601 N Milwaukee Avenue, Wicker Park; stores.barnesandnoble.com

Myopic Books

Many of the aisles at Myopic Books are only wide enough to fit one person at a time; sometimes you even have to turn sideways. Bookshelves seem to have been squeezed in between bookshelves, added out of necessity as the collection expanded, and still many of them bow under their books' weight. Passages arrive at dead ends. Section labels are just laminated pieces of paper tacked to shelves. You're constantly at risk of bumping your head. It is, in sum, a purist's used bookstore, living up to its name in its singular focus on books and nothing but.

☞ 1564 N Milwaukee Avenue, Wicker Park; myopicbookstore.com

Library of Congress

Washington, D.C.

US | NORTH AMERICA

Though Washington, D.C., teems with politicos talking and tweeting, America's capital city also pays tribute to the written word via the world's largest library, a booming bookstore scene, and unexpected literary museums and sites.

If you stacked all of the books in Washington, D.C.'s Library of Congress end to end, they would stretch for 840 miles (1,350 km). It's an apt visual for the capital of the US, which likely ranks as the country's largest repository of literature, showcased both in grand museums and on bookstore shelves. Arguably, Washington, D.C., has gained such a status primarily *because* it's the country's capital. But D.C. is literary in its own right, too. A cadre of prominent names in poetry and prose have spent time here over the centuries. New Yorker Walt Whitman wrote hundreds of poems in D.C. while volunteering at a Civil War hospital and working as a government bureaucrat in the 1800s. Members of the Harlem Renaissance *(p.17)*, such as poet and playwright Langston Hughes and novelist Zora Neale Hurston, also passed through, the latter as an undergrad at the city's Howard University, where she cofounded the student newspaper.

You can give a nod to the greats in the capital's many museums and libraries. Or look to future stars: it's folks like legal thriller novelist David Baldacci and kid-lit icon Jason Reynolds who rule the local scene today—spot their work in buzzing local bookstores.

GETTING AROUND

Compact Washington, D.C., is one of America's most walkable cities and many literary sites are a short stroll from the US Capitol. There's also an expansive subway and bus system.

READING LIST

Red, White & Royal Blue

Casey McQuiston

Alex Claremont-Diaz, the president's son, falls in love with the British Prince Henry in this beloved LGBTQ+ romance novel.

Creatures of Passage

Morowa Yejidé

Long-listed for the Women's Prize for Fiction 2022, Yejidé's haunting *Creatures of Passage* weaves together tales of both the living and the dead.

Heartburn

Nora Ephron

Ephron's wit-filled autobiographical novel is based on her marriage to and divorce from her second husband, Carl Bernstein. The book is set in D.C., where the couple lived together.

Barnes & Noble

Bookstores in landmark buildings are always exciting, and Georgetown's B&N is no exception. This branch of the iconic chain occupies the former home of the first Henry Ford car dealership in the D.C. area. The building, which dates from 1929, still has an industrial feel to it—spacious, airy floors are dotted with concrete pillars and framed by exposed ceilings—but that doesn't mean it isn't welcoming. Stop by for an author talk, a friendly book club, or a chat with the literature-loving staff.

☞ 3040 M Street NW, Georgetown; stores.barnesandnoble.com

Kramers

For generations (well, since 1976), Washingtonians hungry for a good read and a decent dinner have gathered at this Dupont Circle bookstore-meets-café. Lured in by its iconic neon-red sign, they've been quickly wooed by the front table heaped with new releases, and the side bar pouring literary-themed cocktails. (Maybe you're drinking a Pear & Prejudice with St. Germain, pear nectar, and bubbles?) A recent expansion beefed up Kramers' stock of cookbooks and children's literature. But much of the shop remains true to its roots: this is still where locals meet a date for coffee or grab lunch with their book club.

☞ 1517 Connecticut Avenue NW, Dupont Circle; kramers.com

Library of Congress

Created in 1800 by President John Adams with $5,000 for "the purchase of such books as may be necessary for the use of Congress," the world's largest library now spans three buildings near the US Capitol and contains more than 25.77 million books. You'll only see a fraction of them on self-guided tours of the Thomas Jefferson Building, the showiest of the trio. The 1897 Beaux-Arts book palace gleams with literature-inspired wall mosaics and plaques inscribed with quotes by the likes of William Shakespeare. Exhibits, meanwhile, showcase wordy treasures such as a Gutenberg Bible; visitors can also briefly walk into the circular Main Reading Room, where scholars pore over rare books (quiet please!).

☞ Thomas Jefferson Building, 10 First Street SE, Capitol Hill; loc.gov

Folger Shakespeare Library

The world's largest collection of Shakespeareana (books, papers, and artifacts related to the Bard) doesn't reside in London *(p.80)* or Shakespeare's Stratford-on-Avon home—it's in Washington, D.C. You can thank Henry Clay Folger, a theater-obsessed industrialist and antique book collector who opened this library in 1932. The original marble building reads Art Deco on the exterior (gilded doors, stylized mosaics of Shakespeare characters) and high Tudor on the inside (a wood-paneled great

BOOK AT BEDTIME

The Willard Hotel

Hunker down in this Downtown hotel *(washington.intercontinental.com)* and you'll be in the company of literary greats such as Emily Dickinson, plus political icons like Martin Luther King Jr., who wrote his "I Have a Dream" speech here.

hall and Elizabethan-style theater, which hosts plays). In 2024, an expansive addition to the building opened with exhibits on Shakespeare's life and a high-tech room showing off the Folger's 82 copies of the *First Folio*, the 1623 publication that gathered all of the Bard's plays into one book.

☞ 201 East Capitol Street SE, Capitol Hill; folger.edu

Capitol Hill Books

Located in a snug row house across from Eastern Market—a popular Victorian-era food market—Capitol Hill Books deals in lots of literature, and what you might call quirk. Thousands of new, used, antique, and rare books neatly pack the shelves and weathered vintage tables, while Post-it notes whimsically delineate sections—for example, "Hemingway in yonder cubby" or "Constitutional crisis lit." It's a fun place to browse, discovering the niche section headers and stumbling upon a range of titles (you're as likely to pick up an obscure 1930s bestseller as you are a recent crime fiction hit here).

☞ 657 C Street SE, Capitol Hill; capitolhillbooks-dc.com

Capitol Hill Books

Politics and Prose

In a brainy city like D.C., authors are akin to rockstars. How else to explain the crowds packing the nearly nightly readings and literary talks (most of them free) at the three locations of this long-running indie? The original and largest branch, in D.C.'s northwest quadrant, fills a two-level shopfront with novels (not just political tomes, mind), international magazines, and bookish gifts. It's also home to The Den, a basement coffee shop and wine bar—come here in the evening and you might spot a politician or pundit gulping down some liquid courage before they read from their latest bestseller upstairs.

☞ 5015 Connecticut Avenue NW, Upper Northwest DC; politics-prose.com

Frederick Douglass National Historic Site

Born enslaved in 1818, abolitionist and author Frederick Douglass escaped and went on to give impassioned speeches against human bondage, and to pen three autobiographies. Cedar Hill, the hilltop Anacostia mansion where he lived from 1877 until his death in 1895, now operates as a museum dedicated to his life. Guided tours of the house and grounds pass Douglass's 1,000-book library and a windowless outbuilding called the "Growlery," where he smoked his pipe and reviewed his papers.

☞ 1411 W Street SE, Anacostia; nps.gov/frdo/index.htm

French Quarter, New Orleans

New Orleans

LOUISIANA, US | NORTH AMERICA

New Orleans is most famous for its food, jazz, and parties. But this Southern city also has a rich literary history, influenced by its blend of cultural traditions and vibrant atmosphere.

For centuries, stories have traveled along the Mississippi River, carried by enslaved people, sung by blues musicians and documented by writers. In New Orleans, where the river meets the sea, these tales converge and cultures meld like a pot of gumbo, giving it a flavor all its own: Creole, Cajun, and a French *joie de vivre* you can almost taste.

New Orleans's literary history is also seasoned with this blend of influences, attracting artists who sought a new way of seeing the world. Mark Twain journeyed the river by steamboat, chronicled in *Life on the Mississippi*. William Faulkner apparently had more fun in New Orleans than anywhere else in the world. And Tennessee Williams found in it a sort of Paris of America, a place that both shocked and inspired him. In the 20th century in particular, authors like these gathered in the French Quarter, drawn by cheap rent, eccentric muses, and a permissive spirit that still fuels free thinking today.

So, while many come to the Big Easy for beads, beignets, and Bourbon Street, the books are equally worthy of your time. Here, between colorful row houses and sultry swamplands, you'll find one of the South's most literary cities, where the stories keep flowing just like the Mississippi.

GETTING AROUND

You can't visit New Orleans without riding a vintage streetcar (yes, there was one named "Desire"). The city runs four streetcar lines, plus buses and river ferries—all navigable using the Le Pass app.

READING LIST

A Confederacy of Dunces

John Kennedy Toole

A tragicomedy set in 1960s New Orleans, this book follows the misadventures of Ignatius J. Reilly in a crusade against the modern age and all its ignorance and vice.

Interview with the Vampire

Anne Rice

This Southern Gothic tale unveils the chilling confessions of Louis, a former plantation owner turned vampire, in a story of danger, love, and loss.

The Awakening

Kate Chopin

Set in New Orleans and on the Gulf Coast, this feminist classic tracks Edna Pontellier as she rejects the restrictive expectations of Victorian marriage and motherhood.

Galatoire's

It's not every day that lunch begins with cocktails and ends with a live jazz parade, but then Galatoire's is no ordinary place to eat. At this 120-year-old bistro, Friday lunch—a multi-hour affair that is as much party as provision—is almost as famous as the cast of characters who have spent time here, including American writers like Truman Capote and Walker Percy. The historic spot was also a favorite of playwright Tennessee Williams, who sent his protagonists Blanche and Stella here for dinner in *A Streetcar Named Desire* and enjoyed many a meal himself seated in the front window overlooking Bourbon Street. Reservations at "his" table have even been put up for auction—but there's hardly a bad seat in the house at Galatoire's, where you can tuck into a warm bowl of gumbo or shrimp *étouffée*.

☞ 209 Bourbon Street, French Quarter; galatoires.com

Galatoire's

The Old Absinthe House

Absinthe and literature have long gone hand in hand. Oscar Wilde claimed it changes the way you see the world, while Hemingway wrote that it "cures everything" in *For Whom the Bell Tolls*. Perhaps they were reminiscing about nights at the Old Absinthe House, a bohemian institution that has hosted everyone from Mark Twain to Aleister Crowley. New Orleans's answer to Paris's Green Hour—when writers gathered in cafés to chase the mythical effects of the "green fairy"—the bar has inspired artists since the 19th century. Order an Absinthe House Frappe, a tonic of absinthe, anisette, and soda water—and if you feel yourself slipping back in time, it's not just the spirit at work. Much of the original 1806 building remains intact, offering a closer look at the French Creole architecture that gives the city so much of its charm.

☞ 240 Bourbon Street, French Quarter; ruebourbon.com/old-absinthe-house

Hotel Monteleone

If the bar at Hotel Monteleone could talk, oh, the stories it would tell. First, there's the bar itself. Designed like a carousel, with marquee lights and seats that slowly rotate around the center, it became an instant icon when it opened in 1949. Then there are the people who drank here, including literary greats who came to sip on Sazeracs and Vieux Carrés (the latter cocktail invented by the lead bartender). Eudora Welty wrote "The Purple Hat" short story while seated at the bar, Ernest Hemingway mentioned it in his short "The Night Before Battle," and Faulkner wrote his magnum opus, *The Sound and the Fury*, while staying at the inn. A spin at the world-famous watering hole doesn't require a booking, but to truly experience the hotel's storied history, bag one of the six literary suites, each honoring a resident author.

☞ 214 Royal Street, French Quarter; hotelmonteleone.com

Faulkner House Books

Faulkner House Books

In 1925, Mississippi-born writer and aspiring poet William Faulkner quietly launched his career while living in a tiny New Orleans apartment, where he scribbled away at his first novel, *Soldiers' Pay*. Today, the front room of the 1840 townhouse has been transformed into a charming bookstore dedicated to rare Southern fiction and poetry. Only six guests are allowed in the shop at once, giving space to browse the curated collection and time for the owner to handpick treasures tailored to your literary leanings.

624 Pirates Alley, French Quarter; faulknerhousebooks.com

AUTHOR PROFILE

William Faulkner

Winner of the Nobel Prize in Literature, Faulkner is often regarded as the greatest writer of Southern literature. Much of his fiction is set in Mississippi (where he spent much of his life), but New Orleans still inspired him—his very first novel, *Soldiers' Pay* (1925), was written here. Faulkner's complex, stream-of-consciousness stories aren't always the easiest to read, but fans will tell you they're well worth the effort.

Garden District Book Shop

Garden District Book Shop

Many writers have called New Orleans's Garden District home: Anne Rice set a novel in her First Street house; F. Scott Fitzgerald rented an apartment here while editing *This Side of Paradise*, and Walt Whitman stayed nearby during a brief stint in the parish. It's only natural, then, that one of the city's most beloved bookstores would sit among the neighborhood's tree-lined streets and antebellum mansions. Take the St. Charles streetcar—the oldest operating line in the world—to the Garden District Book Shop, an airy space specializing in Louisiana literature. Where most bookstores serve tea and lattes, this one has a full bar (it is New Orleans, after all). Escape the bayou heat with a Vampire's Kiss or a Vronsky's Mock Mule—yes, each muse-worthy cocktail is inspired by either a book or a literary quote.

☞ 2727 Prytania Street Suite 8, Garden District; gardendistrictbookshop.com

BK Historic House and Gardens

Nestled within patinated brick walls and manicured gardens, this New Orleans mansion is a haven for both art and architecture lovers. Built in 1826, the historic home was saved from disrepair in 1945 by author Frances Parkinson Keyes, who later set her novel *The Chess Players* within its halls and was also known to write about the home's colorful former residents in her stories. Today, guided tours offer a glimpse into Keyes's manuscripts, letters, and collection of rare porcelain teapots, while events such as book signings and live storytelling sessions nurture the city's creative spirit.

☞ 1113 Chartres Street, French Quarter; bkhouse.org

Lafayette Cemetery No. 1

Dubbed "cities of the dead," New Orleans cemeteries are known for their above-ground tombs, an eerie and at times beautiful response to life below sea level. In these mazes of mausoleums, horror writer Anne Rice found inspiration for her sensual Gothic style, showcased in her first novel, *Interview with the Vampire*, which would come to redefine the genre itself. At Lafayette Cemetery No. 1, the oldest of seven city-operated graveyards, you'll be haunted by images of the vampire Lestat emerging from a cast-iron crypt, or the Mayfair witches resting beneath a row of spooky crosses. Not one to let her characters steal the spotlight, Rice once staged a mock jazz funeral for herself at the cemetery, riding in a glass coffin to her book signing at the Garden District Book Shop.

☞ 1427 Washington Avenue, Garden District; nola.gov

Milton H. Latter Memorial Library

At first glance, it's hard to believe the Milton H. Latter Memorial Library is part of the public library system. The 1907 Neo-Romanesque mansion, with its wrought-iron balconies and towering live oaks, looks straight out of a Southern romance novel—but here, the devotion is to reading. The Latter family gifted the once-private home to the city in honor of their son, Milton, who was killed in World War II. Much of the original decor remains: students study at stately dining tables, newspapers rest on mahogany desks, and former parlors serve as reading rooms, illuminated by sparkling chandeliers and cozy fireplaces. There are more than 50,000 titles to check out—all you need is a library card.

5120 St. Charles Avenue, Uptown; nolalibrary.org

LITERARY FESTIVAL

Tennessee Williams & New Orleans Literary Festival

This March festival blends books and *bon temps*, luring literature lovers to the city for workshops, food, music and—in honor of its namesake—a raucous "Stella!" shouting contest.

Milton H. Latter Memorial Library

Seattle Central Library

Seattle

WASHINGTON, US | NORTH AMERICA

There are only two UNESCO Cities of Literature in the US, and Seattle is one of them. Washington state's Emerald City doesn't just accommodate book lovers, it's built for them (although this low-key city would hardly ever brag about it).

Seattle's literary culture thrives in the mist. This city in the Pacific Northwest is known for its damp climate and (perhaps as a result) introspective atmosphere. Yet neither is a bad thing for book lovers. The dark clouds drive readers indoors to a sea of independent bookstores, while the grungy music and gallons of coffee fuel the writers of tomorrow. Readings and open-mic nights are also key to the city's culture, with most events happening at Hugo House, named for local poet Richard Hugo.

And you can't talk about literary Seattle without mentioning poetry. The oral and storytelling cultures of the Duwamish and Coast Salish peoples have long infused this land with verse. More recently, University of Washington writing programs have drawn in new voices, including famed poets Theodore Roethke and Carolyn Kizer. And then came the Beats: Gary Snyder and Jack Kerouac worked at fire lookouts near Seattle, writing poetic prose about their time in the wild.

For decades, these Indigenous, intellectual, and bohemian countercultural influences have converged into a unique literary spirit. Reading and writing permeates every neighborhood here, and if ever a new indie pops up, liberal and literary-loving Seattleites will proudly brave the rain to support it.

GETTING AROUND

Buy an Orca card to access Seattle's public streetcars, light rail, buses, and ferries, or find one of the Lime or Bird stations conveniently located all over the city to rent an e-bike or scooter.

READING LIST

Where'd You Go, Bernadette

Maria Semple

When her mother disappears, the teenage Bee pieces together emails, letters, and documents to track her whereabouts, uncovering secrets along the way.

Hotel on the Corner of Bitter and Sweet

Jamie Ford

Spanning decades, this novel tells the story of a Chinese American boy and a Japanese American girl, tracing their lives before, during, and after World War II.

The Boys in the Boat

Daniel James Brown

This nonfiction narrative follows the University of Washington rowing team from Seattle as they strive for Olympic gold in 1936.

Open Books: A Poem Emporium

It's no wonder that Seattle, the city of poets, is home to one of the US's only shops dedicated entirely to verse. This tiny poetry paradise houses thousands of volumes spanning centuries and continents, from ancient epics to experimental zines and chapbooks. Here, you're just as likely to stumble upon a rare first edition or out-of-print poetry book as you are to discover your new favorite Pacific Northwest contemporary voice. The cozy shop hosts regular readings that pack poets shoulder to shoulder, and has a rentable writing parlor; the latter is equipped with a vintage feel (think dark-wood furniture and a patterned rug) and all the "scribbling essentials" you'd ever need. Don't be surprised if you walk in a reader and leave a poet.

☞ 108 Cherry Street, Pioneer Square; open-books-a-poem-emporium.myshopify.com

Blue Moon Tavern

Seattle poets Richard Hugo, Carolyn Kizer, Theodore Roethke, and David Wagoner walk into a bar. No joke—this actually happened at the Blue Moon Tavern, a favorite haunt of the city's literary elite, wayward beatniks like Allen Ginsberg, and the bohemians like Tom Robbins who succeeded them. The tavern isn't exactly a quiet place for reading, but it's an unlikely literary institution with serious credentials. Why? The location. Sitting exactly 1 mile (1.5 km) from the University of Washington, the Blue Moon Tavern marked the legally required minimum distance between a school and a pub in the post-Prohibition era—close enough for leading intellectuals and artists to stumble home. Come here to drink a pint of the city's poetic past, or just enjoy the live music.

☞ 712 NE 45th Street, University District; thebluemoonseattle.com

Seattle Central Library

Designed by Dutch architect Rem Koolhaas, the Seattle Central Library is an architectural marvel. This 11-story structure is famed for its angular glass-and-steel exterior, which reflects the surrounding buildings, and its innovative "book spiral"; winding between four floors, this continuous, wheelchair-accessible ramp showcases the entire nonfiction collection. Other highlights include the Jane Narver Reading Room on the 10th floor, where you can catch a scenic view over Elliott Bay (and see the Elliott Bay Book Company from above). Dizzied by the prospect of exploring the library on your own? Free guided tours are available on weekdays, upon request. Rather explore with friends? Join aspiring writers at the library's jam-packed schedule of free readings and workshops.

☞ 1000 Fourth Avenue, Downtown; spl.org/hours-and-locations/central-library

Elliott Bay Book Company

Beware: once you enter the Elliott Bay Book Company, you may find little reason to leave. Many consider this spot to be the best independent bookstore in Seattle, which is saying a lot in a city with more than 60 bookstores and counting. Despite its vast size—it's housed in an old industrial building—the shop still manages to have a homey, welcoming feel, with rows of wooden shelves crammed with more than 150,000 titles. Browse the near-endless collection of books; hunker down with a locally roasted coffee in the café (tucked at the back of the shop); or catch one of the regular author events, featuring debut novelists, beloved local writers, and seasoned award-winners. There really is no reason to leave.

☞ 1521 10th Avenue, Capitol Hill; elliottbaybook.com

Left Bank Books Collective

Left Bank Books Collective

Calling all radicals and revolutionaries: Left Bank Books is where it's at. This tiny bookstore in Pike Place Market offers an impressive selection of new and used titles with an antiauthoritarian tilt. Its progressive credentials run deep: the shop itself is operated as an anarchist collective, with all decisions made communally. Inside the poster-plastered area are over 10,000 books, focusing on topics as diverse as poetry, queer studies, and critical race theory. More bookish delights await nearby, including the BLMF Literary Saloon (a cheekily named bookstore; if your grandma is out of earshot, ask the staff what BLMF stands for).

92 Pike Street Unit B, Downtown; leftbankbooks.com

BOOK AT BEDTIME

Hotel Sorrento

This historic Downtown hotel is perfect for literary visitors *(hotelsorrento.com)*. Have a drink in the Fireside Room, where poets have gathered for over a century, or join one of the silent reading parties, where you can read quietly alongside other book lovers.

MIDDLE EAST STUDIES
MUCKRAKING
STOLEN CONTINENTS
WAR CRIMES
WOMEN'S STUDIES
and more......
PLEASE LEAVE ALL
BOOKS, PACKS,ETC.
AT THE FRONT DESK
MORE BOOKS
DOWNSTAIRS
BARFLY
SHANGHAI
TIM WISE
MR. LUCKY

City Lights

San Francisco

CALIFORNIA, US | NORTH AMERICA

Home of beatniks and bohemians, California's coolest city has long been a place where literature pushes boundaries, writers champion nonconformity, and readers dare to think differently.

Before Silicon Valley and sky-high rent, San Francisco was for the artists. Its heart-pumping hills, misty mornings, and foggy wharves have long held the allure of the Golden Coast—a horizon that beckoned immigrants and East Coasters with the promise of a new life. But this isn't Los Angeles, with its sheen and stardom. San Francisco was built on grittier dreams: gold in the hills, love in the streets, and flowers in the hair.

Here, Jack London wrote of the frontier, Armistead Maupin told tales of the city's eccentric inhabitants, and John Steinbeck spent his "attic days" before he became a luminary storyteller. The cornerstone of San Francisco's literary reputation? The Beat Generation, a group of rambling writers who congregated in jazz clubs and cafés, rejecting conformity and shaping the counterculture that would come to define the city itself. The Summer of Love in the neighborhood of Haight-Ashbury, the psychedelic rock of the 1960s, even the current tech boom were all born from this ethos of individuality and innovation. So, if you're going to San Francisco, expect to find more than literary landmarks; you'll encounter a spirit that still inspires the poets, pioneers and revolutionaries of today.

GETTING AROUND

San Francisco has an extensive public transportation system, which includes its storybook-worthy cable cars and trolleys. It's also a rewarding place to wander, though be prepared for lots of hills.

READING LIST

On the Road

Jack Kerouac

This beatnik book chronicles two friends' journey across North America in their quest for knowledge and experience. San Francisco features prominently as a city of freedom and fun.

The Joy Luck Club

Amy Tan

Following four Chinese women and their American-born daughters, this novel explores the immigrant experience in the city.

Slouching Towards Bethlehem

Joan Didion

A collection of journalistic essays that paint a portrait of California during the 1960s, particularly focused on the hippie counterculture of the Haight-Ashbury district.

Caffe Trieste

City Lights

At first glance, City Lights might look like the quintessential bookstore: arched doorways, warm lighting and charming corners stacked high with paperbacks. But look a little closer and you'll find something truly countercultural. Founded by poet Lawrence Ferlinghetti in 1953, the shop quickly became a "literary meeting place" where young intellectuals gathered and some of the best minds of the generation were given a voice through its publishing company. Allen Ginsberg's *Howl and Other Poems* was the most famous of its titles, a controversial work that led to the bookstore being raided, staff members arrested, and Ferlinghetti put on trial for obscenity. Despite persecution, he never backed down, and the shop continues to champion progressive authors, banned books, and revolutionary ideas today.

☞ 261 Columbus Avenue, North Beach; citylights.com

Caffe Trieste

North Beach isn't just the birthplace of the Beats; it's also San Francisco's Little Italy, teeming with trattorias, delis, and coffee shops. At Caffe Trieste, you'll find a blend of both worlds: a popular writers' den and the first espresso café on the West Coast. When the Giotta family opened the shop in 1956, the usual suspects—Ginsberg, Ferlinghetti, Kerouac—poured in, along with the likes of poet laureate Jack Hirschman, musician Bob Dylan, and director Francis Ford Coppola, who wrote *The Godfather* screenplay here. Notoriety aside, Caffe Trieste has everything you want in an Italian coffee bar: an old-world aura, eccentric regulars, and little round tables where sunlight streams over macchiatos and manuscripts, meant to be savored slowly.

☞ 601 Vallejo Street, North Beach; caffetrieste.com

Vesuvio Cafe

In 1955, writer Neal Cassady, the inspiration for *On the Road*'s Dean Moriarty, stopped into the saloon across the alley from City Lights and christened it an epicenter of bohemian nightlife. Soon after, Kerouac, Ginsberg, and other members of the Beat Generation were congregating at Vesuvio for jazz, chess, and lively conversation about even livelier ideas. The façade alone makes an impression: a naked figure sipping a martini graces its neon sign, and the exterior wall is hand-painted with vibrant colors and snippets of poetry. Indoors, you'll find vintage Tiffany lamps, more art than should fit on the walls, and drinks that cost less than you'd expect, given the bar's literary pedigree. Grab a spot in the second-story loft for a bird's-eye view of the bar below, and watch the bustling crowd of tourists, artists, and modern-day hipsters continue the conversation started years ago.

☞ 255 Columbus Avenue, North Beach; vesuvio.com

Green Apple Books

Founded in 1967, Green Apple Books is a bit like that closet you keep meaning to clean out—overflowing shelves and curated treasures hidden beneath the chaos. The experience begins on the sidewalk, where carts of books hunker under the shop's green awning. They offer just a preview of the 60,000 new and 100,000 used titles packed inside. Also inside? Handwritten signs showcasing the staff's humor and quirky touches like a book recommendation dispenser. Community is at Green Apple's core, and this shop feel wonderfully lived in.

☞ 506 Clement Street, Richmond District; greenapplebooks.com

San Francisco Public Library

You might know Maya Angelou for her award-winning poetry and advocacy, but she also has a lesser-known claim to fame: at just 16 years old, she became San Francisco's first Black female streetcar conductor. Now, a bronze portrait honoring her legacy stands outside San Francisco Public Library. Much of the library was destroyed in the 1906 earthquake (some 140,000 volumes were lost), but today it's one of the most vibrant systems in the country. It has a deep commitment to the city's residents, with collections spanning 50 languages and a bookmobile delivering resources to underserved communities.

☞ 100 Larkin Street, Civic Center; sfpl.org

Green Apple Books

John's Grill

In the popular 1930 novel *The Maltese Falcon*, hard-boiled detective Sam Spade wanders the streets of San Francisco in search of a jewel-encrusted falcon—and, it seems, a meal at John's Grill, the historic steakhouse that opened in 1908. Now a literary landmark, this atmospheric restaurant evokes a bygone era with its white tablecloths, leather banquettes and dark-wood walls; it's no mystery why author Dashiell Hammett chose it for his noir classic. Head upstairs to the Maltese Falcon Room to spot a statue of the eponymous bird and nosh on the grill's signature lamb chops with potatoes and sliced tomatoes. For years, Hammett worked at the detective agency next door, and his 891 Post Street apartment (also Spade's address) stood right around the corner, leaving you wondering how much of the book is fact and how much is fiction.

John's Grill

63 Ellis Street, Union Square; johnsgrill.com

The Mechanics' Institute Library

Housed in a 1910 Beaux-Arts building, the San Francisco Mechanics' Institute is home to the country's oldest chess club and one of the West Coast's oldest libraries. Grab a day pass to the members-only library and climb the shell-like spiral staircase to the two-story reading room, where soaring columns, floor-to-ceiling windows, and plush leather chairs invite you to stay a while (with more than 160,000 items in the collection, losing track of time isn't hard here). Mechanics' Institutes began in 19th-century Scotland as educational hubs for working-class men; in San Francisco, the institution served out-of-work miners from the Gold Rush. As one of only three remaining Mechanics' Institutes in the US, this cultural center continues to enrich the lives of everyday people through after-hours talks, movie screenings, and writers' groups—many of them open to the public.

57 Post Street, Financial District; milibrary.org

Black Bird Bookstore

Great books and great coffee await at Black Bird Bookstore. This cozy Sunset spot is beloved by its community, particularly local families—there's comfy seating where parents can take a breather, and kid-friendly nooks where children can read. The bookshelves also have plenty of picture books and YA titles, as well as a curated selection of adult titles. Better yet, there's a coffee shop and a leafy patio where you can sit and sip your flavored latte.

4541 Irving Street, Outer Sunset; blackbirdsf.com

Fabulosa Books

Fabulosa Books

San Francisco played a critical role in the advancement of LGBTQ+ rights. It was the first city in the US to allow gay couples to legally marry, and it was home to the state's first openly gay elected official and the birthplace of the iconic rainbow flag. While Fabulosa Books might be a newcomer as of 2021, the little purple shop is part of a long history of queer pride in the Castro neighborhood. As well as stocking plenty of LGBTQ+ titles, the shop is also an advocate for LGBTQ+ folks in less-welcoming parts of the country through "Books Not Bans," a customer-funded program that donates affirming literature to places where LGBTQ+ stories have been silenced.

489 Castro Street, The Castro; fabulosabooks.com

BOOK AT BEDTIME

Hotel Emblem

Located in the Theater District, Hotel Emblem *(hotelemblem.com)* is perfect for book lovers. Have a good read delivered to your room by the inn's Book Butler, or have a good time at the Obscenity Bar, named for the Ferlinghetti trial.

The Salinas Valley

Steinbeck Country

CALIFORNIA, US | NORTH AMERICA

Two hours south of San Francisco, the Bay Area gives way to the rural farm towns of the Salinas Valley and the coastal hamlet of Monterey. Here, in this 90-mile (145-km) stretch of fertile ground, American author John Steinbeck was born and raised. Though he later moved on to other cities, the Salinas Valley remained his ever-present muse, an Edenic land that became the backdrop for his epic allegories and working-class sagas.

At the turn of the 20th century, John Steinbeck spent his formative years in California's farm country, roaming the region's hills and working as a ranch hand alongside migrant laborers. These early experiences connected him deeply to the land and the struggles of everyday people, whose stories he illuminated in novels like *The Grapes of Wrath* and *Of Mice and Men*. More than a literary setting, Steinbeck's country became a character in and of itself, brought to life through his sensory descriptions of the valley's "sometimes river" and "beckoning mountains with a brown grass love."

Where lettuce sprouts beneath the Gabilan Mountains, and artichokes flourish along the shimmering coast, book lovers will find a bounty of sites associated with Steinbeck's life, from the real Cannery Row to his childhood home.

BOOKISH PLACES

National Steinbeck Center

In the heart of downtown Salinas, this museum contains the world's largest collection of Steinbeck artifacts, with more than 45,000 letters, manuscripts, and photos from the author's life.

steinbeck.org

Cannery Row

This famous street on Monterey Bay was the setting for Steinbeck's novel of the same name. Now it's a bustling tourism district, but you can still spot the historic Ed Ricketts lab and a statue of the acclaimed author.

canneryrow.com

Steinbeck House

On his 72nd birthday, Steinbeck's boyhood home was transformed into a restaurant that showcases produce from the Salinas Valley. Dishes are named after some of his most beloved novels, and tours of the 1897 Victorian house are offered monthly.

steinbeckhouse.com

John Steinbeck's Grave

Pay tribute at the final resting place of John Steinbeck and the Hamilton side of his family—the real-life inspiration for *East of Eden*'s multigenerational cast of characters.

850 Abbott Street, Salinas

John Steinbeck

Vancouver Public Library

Vancouver

CANADA | NORTH AMERICA

Outdoorsy Vancouver might not be on every bibliophile's radar, but it should be. This cool Canadian city has all the inspiration (snowcapped peaks, rolling waves) and information (top-notch libraries, indie bookstores) readers and writers could want.

With streets that stretch from the Pacific Ocean through dense forests and up to lofty mountain peaks, this breezy coastal city is famed for its postcard-perfect scenery. But Vancouver isn't a book you should judge by its cover. Spend a little more time in Canada's west-coast capital and you'll discover there's more to the story than meets the eye.

Vancouver has long been literary. This is where Nobel laureate Alice Munro—Canada's first woman to win the Booker Prize—crafted her short stories in the 1950s. Where, a few decades later, local cult novelist Douglas Coupland immortalized the city's quirks in *City of Glass*. And where Indigenous roots and diasporic voices line the shelves of a thriving network of indie bookstores, telling the city's stories from a range of perspectives—Michelle Good's *Five Little Indians* and Joy Kogawa's *Obasan* are among the local favorites.

The stats tell their own story. Consistently ranking among Canada's most well-read cities and boasting one of the highest library circulation rates in the country, Vancouver's locals have powered through paperbacks and bolstered the city's literary credentials. Join them in their city library, at a poetry slam, or simply enjoying the outdoors, a good book always in hand.

GETTING AROUND

Biking in Vancouver isn't just a way to get around, it's a way of life. So, download the Mobi app to access the public bike-share network and explore this scenic city on two wheels.

READING LIST

The Love of a Good Woman

Alice Munro

This collection of linked short stories explores the hidden desires, moral dilemmas, and intimate lives of its characters, capturing the subtleties of city and suburban life.

JPod

Douglas Coupland

A satirical, fast-paced novel following a quirky group of young video game designers as they navigate working life.

Five Little Indians

Michelle Good

Good's powerful novel follows the lives of five Indigenous survivors of Canada's residential schools, examining their trauma and the challenges of reclaiming identity in a modern city.

Vancouver Public Library

When in Rome, do as the Romans do. But when in the Roman Colosseum–inspired Vancouver Public Library, do as the Vancouverites do: bring your book up to the ninth floor's rooftop garden to take in city views. Sprawling across an entire city block known as "Library Square," Vancouver's central downtown library branch is housed in an architectural marvel, beloved by literary and design aficionados alike. Out-of-town travelers can snag lending privileges with a simple visitor's card purchase, and can access the packed calendar of free events. When your two-for-one book-and-building tour feels complete, quench your thirst downstairs at the aptly named Library Square Pub, where you can toast your borrowed book haul with a local craft brew.

☞ 350 West Georgia Street, Downtown; vpl.ca

Massy Books

Musqueam, Squamish, and Tsleil-Waututh: these are the names of the three Indigenous Nations upon whose traditional territory the city of Vancouver is located. This context matters to understand why Massy Books—one of the few 100 percent Indigenous-owned bookstores—is both notable and well worth a visit. Located in Chinatown, this fiercely independent gem is celebrated in the community for platforming Indigenous authors, alongside the voices of writers too often marginalized by the colonial canon. The curation here is intentional, powerful, and political, creating an impact that far outsizes the shop's compact brick-and-mortar footprint. Patricia Massy, the Nêhiyaw-Métis shop founder, is also one of the minds behind Indigenous Brilliance—a collective with events empowering Indigenous storytellers, many of which are hosted in the shop. Insider tip: look out for the secret bookshelf door that leads into a children's reading room.

☞ 229 E Georgia Street, Chinatown; massybooks.com

Upstart & Crow

Upstart & Crow isn't simply a bookstore. This cool indie is beloved for its well-stocked shelves and old-school rolling ladders (the main character in everyone's photos). But what ordinary visitors might not realize is that it doubles as a nonprofit, funding residencies for BIPOC writers, climate crisis communicators, and poets. It's also known for hosting community workshops that turn readers into writers. The best part? You'll have to travel to Granville Island, Vancouver's artistic epicenter, to find it. While here, be sure to visit Nooroongji, a nearby multilingual bookstore, and pop into Paper-Ya to stock up on unusual stationery from around the world. Time it right and you'll arrive in time for the iconic Vancouver Writer's Fest, which takes over Granville Island's theaters in October.

☞ 1387 Railspur Alley, Granville Island; upstartandcrow.com

MacLeod's Books

Remember that 1984 fantasy film *The NeverEnding Story*? The one where a kid hides out in a bookstore to escape the bullies at school? MacLeod's Books is that bookstore—and it's just as mythical as it's made out to be in the film. Nothing seems to have changed since the 1980s, which is a large part of the shop's charm. Holding its ground smack dab in the middle of Vancouver's ever-modernizing downtown core, MacLeod's is exactly what you imagine a used bookstore to be: a topsy-turvy maze with more hardcovers piled on the ground than on the shop's shelves, tons of quirky character, and the musty aroma of well-turned pages. Come here for the city's best selection of rare and antiquarian books, or to simply relive the film.

☞ 455 W Pender Street, Downtown; 604-681-7654

Historic Joy Kogawa House

Though World War II never made it to Canadian soil, it still had a devastating effect—especially on Japanese Canadian immigrants who were forced into internment camps across British Columbia. Joy Kogawa, born in Canada to Japanese parents, was one of them. She tells her story in *Obasan*, her seminal novel published in 1981, which built momentum for her to become one of the leading voices asking the Canadian government to apologize and provide reparations for those affected. Today, Kogawa's legacy is memorialized at the Historic Joy Kogawa House, located in her childhood home.

1450 W 64th Avenue, Marpole; kogawahouse.com

AUTHOR PROFILE

Alice Munro

Alice Munro lived the librarian-turned-author story that most writers dream of. Before becoming the first Canadian woman to win the Nobel Prize in Literature, she lived a humble life, working at the Kitsilano Public Library. She then opened the famed indie Munro's Books on Vancouver Island in 1963 (it's still going strong today). A couple of years later, she published her first short story collection.

Upstart & Crow

L. M. Montgomery's Birthplace

Prince Edward Island

CANADA | NORTH AMERICA

If you've heard of Prince Edward Island (PEI), you may have already met Anne. L. M. Montgomery's 1908 children's classic, Anne of Green Gables, *put this charming Canadian island firmly on the literary map. Today, "Anne tourism" still draws devoted readers from around the world to experience the real-life setting that inspired the international bestseller. Step ashore and you'll swear you've walked straight into the story.*

Green Gables Heritage Place

Formerly owned by Montgomery's cousins, this green-gabled farmstead has been restored and is now a re-creation of Anne's home in the book.

parks.canada.ca/lhn-nhs/pe/greengables

Anne of Green Gables Museum

L. M. Montgomery's aunt and uncle's pretty house is now the Anne Museum, housing Montgomery memorabilia and artifacts that inspired the book.

annemuseum.com

L. M. Montgomery's Birthplace

Fans can visit the home where Montgomery was born to see relics from her life—including her scrapbooks and a replica of her wedding gown—and explore the sand dunes nearby, featured in her other novels.

lmmontgomerybirthplace.ca

Avonlea Village

This quaint themed village replicates the fictional Avonlea, complete with Anne-themed shops.

avonlea.ca

More than a century after it was published, *Anne of Green Gables* remains one of Canada's most beloved stories. The coming-of-age classic follows protagonist Anne, a spirited orphan—sporting iconic red-haired pigtails—who comes to live in the Cuthberts' "green-gabled" farmhouse. The book is set in the fictional town of Avonlea, which was inspired by the PEI town of Cavendish, where Montgomery grew up.

The author wrote 20 novels and hundreds of short stories, but it was Anne who made her a Person of National Historic Significance in Canada in 1943. Visiting PEI still means walking through her world—the places she grew up are open to fans and the landscapes that inspired her (wind-whipped coasts and red-dirt roads) are free to explore. Just try not to be *too* inspired by Anne and all her misadventures.

Lucy Maud Montgomery

Biblioteca Vasconcelos

Mexico City

MEXICO | NORTH AMERICA

Bookish places in Mexico City are far from ordinary. Step into Mexico's sprawling capital and you'll discover gorgeous, design-led bookstores, completely unique libraries, and a host of fascinating cultural spaces dedicated to local authors.

Back in 1539, the first book in the Americas was printed in Mexico City—and the Mexican capital has been obsessed with books ever since. This is where revolutionary poet Sor Juana Inés de la Cruz challenged the establishment from her convent cell, where Nobel laureate Octavio Paz lived and wrote, and where Carlos Fuentes captured the contradictions of modern Mexico in novels like *Where the Air Is Clear*. Many authors have used the city—with its blend of Aztec ruins, colonial architecture, and modern constructions—as a setting, including Gonzalo Celorio in the coming-of-age novel *Amor propio* and Guillermo Fadanelli in the thriller *Hotel DF*. Today, acclaimed contemporary writers like Valeria Luiselli and Brenda Navarro continue to draw inspiration from—and capture the essence of—the modern metropolis.

And no wonder they're so inspired: take a stroll here and you'll see the city's bookish obsession everywhere. Impressive public libraries are filled with centuries-old tomes and floating bookshelves; cultural centers and mansions pay homage to local writers; and an array of bookstores provides endless options for your next read. It looks like Mexico City's love of literature isn't going anywhere.

GETTING AROUND

Base yourself in Coyoacán or Condesa for walkable bookish neighborhoods, or the Centro Histórico for easy access to Calle Donceles and major libraries. The Metro is efficient and cheap.

READING LIST

Horizontal Vertigo: A City Called Mexico

Juan Villoro

Part memoir, part cultural history, this book captures the sprawl of Mexico City, moving through its neighborhoods to build an intimate portrait of life in the capital.

The Story of My Teeth

Valeria Luiselli

This playful and unconventional novel follows an eccentric auctioneer, using humor and digression to explore storytelling, value, and the city's shifting cultural margins.

Where the Air Is Clear

Carlos Fuentes

This Modernist work follows the rise and fall of financier Federico Robles, weaving multiple voices to capture the capital's social divisions, history, and restless energy.

Biblioteca Vasconcelos

Few public buildings have been photographed as much as this library, and you'll see why as soon as you step inside. Conceived by Mexican architect Alberto Kalach, this architectural marvel has six floors of futuristic steel bookshelves that seemingly float in mid-air above the central hall. Making the space even more impressive is *Matrix Móvil*, artist Gabriel Orozco's gray whale skeleton—a piece so striking it once traveled to New York's Museum of Modern Art. Natural light floods the space (the design cleverly prevents it from damaging the collection of 600,000 books), with reading nooks and balconies on the upper floors overlooking the library and the city. Needless to say, book lovers adore the place, and even regulars still get captivated by the architecture.

☞ Eje 1 Norte S/N, Cuauhtémoc; bibliotecavasconcelos.gob.mx

Biblioteca Vasconcelos

Biblioteca de México

This 18th-century building lived many lives—tobacco factory, prison, hospital—before opening as a library in 1946. Today it's home to some of Mexico's oldest and most treasured books, with volumes dating back to the 1500s, some with rare bindings in unusual materials (like snakeskin). But the real draw is the personal libraries of five prominent Mexican intellectuals, including renowned chronicler Carlos Monsiváis. Compiled in 2011 by Mexico's Secretary of Culture in a project called La Ciudad de los Libros (The City of Books), these collections are housed in separate rooms designed to honor their old owners; for instance, in Monsiváis's room, the shelves were inspired by Mexico City's architecture (as he wrote so much about the capital). Visually stunning, the collections are considered one of the great cultural achievements of 21st-century Mexico.

☞ Plaza de la Ciudadela #4, Cuauhtémoc; bibliotecademexico.gob.mx

Calle Donceles

Dozens of used bookstores line both sides of this street in the historic center, but they all trace back to one man. In the 1930s, Nicolás López Casillas started buying used books in Tepito, a neighborhood famous for its gritty street market, to resell. Over the years, his family opened eight bookstores on Calle Donceles, one of the city's oldest streets, established in 1524. Their flagship, Librería Regia, is still family-owned and houses more than a million volumes. Other notable stops include Bibliofilia and Librería El Laberinto, though collectors often find their best discoveries by simply wandering. As you browse, expect to uncover everything from cheap encyclopedias to first editions of Gabriel García Márquez and Agatha Christie; most books are in Spanish, but there are a few English titles, too.

☞ Calle Donceles, Centro Histórico

Centro Cultural Elena Garro

Casa Rivas Mercado

This eclectic mansion mixes Moorish mosaics, Victorian woodwork, Art Nouveau ironwork, and Classical columns into an architectural experiment. Architect Antonio Rivas Mercado built it in the 1890s, and it became a gathering place for the city's intellectuals, writers and artists. His daughter Antonieta grew up here before becoming a cultural force: polyglot writer, feminist, and promoter of what's now the National Symphony Orchestra. Today, the house is a museum dedicated to her legacy and to women's contributions to Mexican literary and cultural life.

C. Héroes 45, Cuauhtémoc; sic.cultura.gob.mx/ficha.php?table=museo&table_id=2216

Centro Cultural Elena Garro

This cultural center and bookstore presents a striking sight. Architect Fernanda Canales wrapped a concrete-and-glass shell around an early 20th-century mansion, with sculptor Paloma Torres adding patterns to the exposed surfaces. It's a space designed by women, and named after a woman: Elena Garro, a playwright and novelist who was one of Mexico's most important 20th-century writers. Explore the two-level bookstore, which has a strong collection on gender theory, or take in a workshop, talk, or performance in one of the mansion's rooms.

Fernández Leal 43, Coyoacán; sic.cultura.gob.mx/ficha.php?table=centro_cultural&table_id=2665

UNAM Central Library

Art and literature coexist in many of Mexico City's landmarks, but nowhere so prominently as here. Nearly 43,000 sq ft (4,000 sq m) of stone mosaic cover this 10-story library at the National Autonomous University of Mexico, where poet Octavio Paz studied in the 1930s. Opened in 1956, the building's exterior was designed by architect and muralist Juan O'Gorman, who traveled across Mexico collecting over 150 types of naturally colored stones to create art that would last a thousand years. Each side of the building depicts a different era of Mexican history—pre-Hispanic (north), colonial (south), revolutionary (east), and modern (west). The library undoubtedly attracts its fair share of art lovers, but bibliophiles aren't left out: inside, open stacks hold 1.5 million volumes, including rare books from the 15th century.

☞ Escolar S/N, C.U., Coyoacán; bibliotecacentral.unam.mx

El Péndulo

The Polanco branch of this bookstore-café chain feels more like a literary living room than a shop. Split across two floors, the charming shop is lined with heaving bookcases and dotted with plants; sofas are also tucked here and there, where book lovers can curl up with a new read or students can settle in for long conversations over a pot of coffee or tea. Topping things off is the breakfast menu, which includes dishes named after Mexican authors. The shop is in Polanquito, a walkable enclave near Parque Lincoln in swanky Polanco, with a street-level terrace that opens to the neighborhood and quieter corners upstairs for browsing new titles in Spanish and English. Five other locations exist across the city (including Art Deco mansions in Roma and Condesa), but this is the flagship and, some say, the most beautiful.

☞ Alejandro Dumas 81, Miguel Hidalgo; pendulo.com

El Péndulo

Arte universal

Biblioteca Virgilio Barco

Bogotá

COLOMBIA | SOUTH AMERICA

Oft-overlooked, the Colombian capital has long been a land of literary resilience. Today, the city harbors stories born from the ashes of its violent history and displayed in architecturally impressive libraries and cool community bookstores.

Colombia's complicated history has been a catalyst for its great literary output. Forged by centuries of violence, emboldened writers with sharp pens have surfaced from the wound, carving out an astonishing legacy and spearheading numerous literary movements. In the 19th century, Costumbrismo (a love letter to everyday life) and Romanticism ruled, emerging as a result of the newly independent nation's optimism. Then, in the 1950s, Nadaísmo (Nothing-ism) built on the existentialism and social protest that prevailed.

As a hub of creativity, Colombia's capital has also been home to numerous acclaimed writers. José Asunción Silva wrote his masterful *Nocturno* here and later became one of the leaders of Latin American modern poetry. Gabriel García Márquez *(p.68)* also found his voice here, first as a journalist.

Bogotá has been built on the struggles of its past, but this modern, mountainous city has also been busy writing a new chapter in its history. A host of striking libraries appeared on the city skyline in the late 20th and early 21st centuries (highlighting the importance Bogotá places on the written word), while forward-thinking bookstores continue to pop up, preserving the city's cultural legacy and promoting its future.

GETTING AROUND

Bogotá is very bike-friendly—every Sunday, numerous roads close to cars and fill with cyclists (visitors can easily rent bikes from docking stations around the city). Alternatively, ride-sharing apps are popular.

READING LIST

The Sound of Things Falling

Juan Gabriel Vásquez

Much of Colombia's modern literary fiction examines the devastating effects of the violent drug cartels; *The Sound of Things Falling* is one of the best.

Satanás

Mario Mendoza

Inspired by true events, *Satanás* follows Campo Elías Delgado, a troubled war veteran whose psychological instability drives him to become a mass murderer.

Delirio

Laura Restrepo

After Agustina, a woman from an upper-class family in Bogotá, suffers a mental breakdown, her husband searches for answers, uncovering secrets from her past and the city's hidden corruption.

Biblioteca Luis Ángel Arango

Biblioteca Luis Ángel Arango

Located in the heart of La Candelaria, the city's historical center, this megabiblioteca is the biggest and most important library in Colombia. It's a bustling bookish hub, welcoming locals and tourists alike with its vibrant program of events (lectures, workshops, exhibitions, and the like), plus a trove of some 2.7 million books. But perhaps its most fascinating feature is the Sala de Libros Raros. The only space in the city solely devoted to archiving rare on-paper treasures, this hushed, near-holy room preserves original manuscripts dating back to colonial times, the country's first published books, travel logs of voyagers from the 18th century, and first editions of Gabriel García Márquez's iconic masterpieces. It's a veritable trove for researchers.

Calle 11 #4-14, La Candelaria; banrepcultural.org

Gabriel García Márquez Cultural Center

Master of storytelling, icon of magical realism, inspiration for countless writers, pride and joy of an entire nation: meet Gabriel García Márquez. Colombia's most famous author is well-celebrated throughout the country (particularly in his hometown of Aracataca; *p.68*). In Bogotá, this cultural center not only champions his work, it also keeps his legacy alive by forging culture through storytelling. All art forms are given space here (theater, music, and painting) and, as you'd expect, the center is also home to a popular bookstore. You'll find a hefty collection of Ibero-American authors, including an array of books by the center's eponymous literary hero.

Calle 11 #5-60, La Candelaria; +57 128 32200

Biblioteca Virgilio Barco

Words meet nature at Biblioteca Virgilio Barco. Sprawled across Simón Bolívar Metropolitan Park (the green lungs of the city and the largest urban park in Colombia), this innovative library is surrounded by elegant pools of water and calming green spaces. It was designed by famed French Colombian architect Rogelio Salmona to blend in with the leafy surrounds of Bogotá—its snail-shaped building offers both in- and outdoor reading spaces (ideal given the city's changeable weather) and sweeping windows let in tons of light. When the rainy season hits, join the locals scribbling away at desks in the airy reading rooms and hunkering down between the shelves. And when the hot sun returns, head outside: you could take a walk around the gorgeous grounds, catch a show at the open-air theater, or wander up on the winding roof to gaze across the city.

Avenida Carrera 60 #57-60, Teusaquillo; +57 601 5803010

Quevedo Libros y Antigüedades

You never know what you'll find in the House of Second Chances (as this old bookstore has been lovingly nicknamed). Around 50 years' worth of stock has been accumulated within this intimate and wonderfully chaotic maze of narrow corridors. There are dog-eared books, classic records, old magazines, vintage photographs, historic stamps, and even a few odd toys. There's also a staircase (not for sale) decorated with Gabriel García Márquez's painted face and a bunch of yellow butterflies, symbols of his fictional town of Macondo in *One Hundred Years of Solitude*. The best way to explore is to simply get lost and let your eyes wander: they might snag on a hidden, but not entirely forgotten, literary treasure.

Carrera 11 #67–24, Chapinero; +57 310 2089706

Librería Wilborada 1047

An homage to Wiborada, the patron saint of books and librarians and the first woman formally canonized in the year 1047, this bookstore is a haven for bookish souls. Built on Colombian soil, under an English timber-framed roof and named after a Swiss saint, it's also a patchwork of cultures, as are its bookshelves. Stories from all over the world line the attic, the interior bridge-corridors, and the central courtyard. As part of Librería Wilborada 1047's commitment to sharing the love for the written word, staff also host a lively Book Exchange event on the last Sunday of every month. Expect a delicious selection of coffee (for which this country is famous); comfy spaces to read; and a friendly, book-loving crowd who (usually) have great taste in books.

Calle 71 #10–47 Int 4, Chapinero; wilborada1047.com

Matorral Librería

This is no ordinary bookstore, and it never wanted to be. On opening, Matorral Librería aimed to break the intellectual stereotype of other literary hubs by creating a space where everyone would feel welcome. Said space is cute, cozy, and bohemian: picture a spiral staircase in the heart of a woody, treehouse-like space. It's equally enticing in the backyard. This is a place where Bogotá's cool kids hang, drinking coffee and munching on pastries during the day, and sipping on artisanal beer and listening to music come evening. It's all good books and good vibes.

Avenida Carrera 19 #36–55, Teusaquillo; matorral.com.co

Matorral Librería

Mural in Aracataca

Aracataca

COLOMBIA | SOUTH AMERICA

Best known for his 1967 magical realism masterpiece, One Hundred Years of Solitude, *Gabriel García Márquez first found his muse in his birthplace, Aracataca. Located deep in Colombia's Caribbean region and nestled beneath the looming peaks of the Sierra Nevada de Santa Marta, the tiny town now stands as a living, breathing homage to the country's most celebrated author.*

Gabriel García Márquez House Museum

Built as a perfect reconstruction of Gabo's childhood home, where he lived with his grandparents, this building later served as the setting for the Buendías's house in *One Hundred Years of Solitude*.

Carrera 6 Este

Telegraphist's House

The original telegraph office from 1894 is where Gabo's father worked, and where the secret love story between his parents started—the inspiration for *Love in the Time of Cholera*.

Calle 9 #5-30

Macondo Linear Park

This scenic walkway along the riverbank features colorful bridges and over 30 murals painted by regional artists, depicting Gabo-themed scenes.

Carrera 2 Este #3b2

Monument to Remedios la Bella

Portraying Remedios, the most beautiful woman in Macondo, this monument was built in 1992 to celebrate a decade of Gabo's Nobel Prize in Literature win.

Calle 3A #1-51

Although his typewriter was heard in many cities, Gabo (as he's affectionately known in Colombia) kept Aracataca and the people of his past at the heart of every story—"There's nothing that I've written that isn't rooted in reality," he once said. Most famously, details of this land—its fluttering yellow butterflies; its crystal-clear river; and big, white stones—became the inspiration for Macondo, the fictional town in Gabo's epic *One Hundred Years of Solitude*.

Aracataca is like most of Colombia's rural Caribbean towns: small and lovingly sustained by the efforts of its vibrant community. By exploring the landmarks that inspired Gabo and the tributes the locals have paid him over the years, you'll soon realize that even the most ordinary of places can inspire something extraordinary ... even magical.

Gabriel García Márquez

Real Gabinete Português de Leitura

Rio de Janeiro

BRAZIL | SOUTH AMERICA

While Rio de Janeiro is better known for its stunning natural beauty and colorful carnival, the city also has a rich literary heritage, something best seen in its magnificent libraries, fin-de-siècle cafés, and local bookstores.

Rio de Janeiro's literary scene took off at the end of the 19th century, when the gilded interiors of its belle-époque cafés hummed and buzzed with bookish debates. Such literary leanings found formal recognition in 1897 with the establishment of the Brazilian Academy of Letters. Led by Machado de Assis, one of the greatest writers in Brazil's history, its purpose was to promote Brazilian literature and to inspire writers with lectures, debates, and publications.

Rio has taken this creative tradition forward into its modern-day festivals, such as the Reader's Festival, featuring lectures and author meetings, and the biennial Bienal do Livro Rio, one of Brazil's largest book fairs. Other events, meanwhile, amplify voices that were previously overlooked in the city's literary canon; among them is the Festa Literária das Periferias, which offers a platform for writers from Rio's favelas and marginalized communities.

Given such bookish leanings, it's unsurprising that Rio was made a UNESCO City of Literature back in 2023. Today, the city's love of books looms both large and small; here, grand, beautifully designed libraries sit alongside tiny neighborhood bookstores run by passionate locals.

GETTING AROUND

Rio's metro links beachfront neighborhoods such as Copacabana and Ipanema with the historic downtown, where many of the city's libraries, cafés, and bookstores are concentrated.

READING LIST

Dom Casmurro

Machado de Assis

Exploring themes of love, memory, and the ambiguity of truth, this classic novel follows Bentinho, whose obsessive jealousy and suspicion of his wife's infidelity unravels his life.

City of God

Paulo Lins

Based on true events in Rio's notorious favelas, this gritty novel traces the lives of children growing up amid violence, capturing the harsh realities of the city's margins.

The Passion According to G. H.

Clarice Lispector

This compelling philosophical novel, set in a solitary apartment in Rio, sees a woman's encounter with a cockroach lead to acts of both transformation and transgression.

Fundação Biblioteca Nacional

Step into South America's largest library and it's easy to see why Cariocas (Rio locals) take pride in their cultural institutions. Founded in 1810, the Biblioteca Nacional houses around 9 million items, among their number rare manuscripts, early Brazilian imprints, and extensive newspaper archives. While the breadth of the collection is impressive, the Neo-Classical palace it's housed in is even more so. A columned entrance leads into a lofty hall, with a sweeping marble staircase leading to reading rooms that feel more like elegant ballrooms than your standard study halls. A highlight is the main reading room, sitting beneath a vast glass dome, where students and researchers bend studiously over their books. Tours explore both the library's architecture and its literary collection.

☞ Av Rio Branco 219, Centro; bn.gov.br

Livraria da Travessa

Real Gabinete Português de Leitura

This late-19th-century, Neo-Manueline library is home to one of Rio's most astonishing interiors. Here, a black-and-white marble floor, dotted with neat rows of polished wooden desks, rises toward an intricate stained-glass ceiling that floods the space with colored light. Sandwiched between them are three levels of carved dark-wooden shelves packed with countless volumes, including rare editions that sit behind ornate iron galleries. The brainchild of a group of immigrants from Portugal who wanted to showcase their home country's literature, the collection specializes in Portuguese-language books. (In fact, with more than 350,000 items, it's the largest collection of Portuguese works outside Portugal.) Today, it's still a working research library, attracting scholars from around the world—although many visitors come simply to marvel at a space that treats books as objects of reverence.

☞ Rua Luís de Camões 30, Centro; realgabinete.com.br

Livraria da Travessa

Found among the surf shops of beach-obsessed Ipanema, this spacious contemporary bookstore is the flagship shop of Livraria da Travessa, a well-loved chain. Inside, two floors of black bookshelves burst with a wide range of titles, including a strong selection of Brazilian fiction, essays, and criticism. This is a place where lingering is encouraged, whether that's browsing for your next read among the heavily laden shelves or discussing your favorite books in the bright and breezy on-site café. The shop often hosts bookish events, where writers and readers mingle sociably in true Carioca style.

☞ Rua Visconde de Pirajá 572, Ipanema; travessa.com.br

Confeitaria Colombo

Opened in 1894, Confeitaria Colombo is one of Rio's most beautiful belle époque cafés, with an opulent interior decorated by gilded mirrors, stained-glass windows, and crystal chandeliers. At the turn of the century, though, this café was more than a pretty face; it also drew in writers, artists, and politicians eager to debate ideas over coffee and cakes. Some of the city's most famous literary figures, among them poet Olavo Bilac and writer Coelho Neto, would frequent this spot, turning it into an informal outpost of the Brazilian Academy of Letters. Such a reputation was warmly encouraged by Manuel Lebrão, the café's owner, who was known to accept creative forms of payment to settle a bill, including poems. (While the space may inspire you to write a few lines of verse, don't expect a free coffee.)

Rua Gonçalves Dias 32, Centro; confeitariacolombo.com.br

Confeitaria Colombo

Livraria Folha Seca

A narrow street in Rio's historic center, the Rua do Ouvidor was a lively literary hub in the 19th century, home to newspapers, periodicals, and publishers. This bookish tradition continues today with Livraria Folha Seca, a charming bookstore that specializes in books about Rio de Janeiro, with a strong focus on topics such as literature, history, and music. The shop was set up by book lover and devoted soccer fan Rodrigo Ferrari (there are plenty of soccer books on the shelves, too), who has turned it into a welcoming neighborhood hangout for Rio's literary minded. Regulars drop by to browse the shelves and chat to the ever-friendly Ferrari, or to catch an author signing, reading, or book launch—some from authors published by the shop's in-house imprint, Folha Seca. Come evening, expect samba performances and literary debates over beers.

Rua do Ouvidor 37, Centro; livrariafolhaseca.com.br

AUTHOR PROFILE

Machado de Assis

Born in Rio de Janeiro to a working-class family, Machado de Assis became one of Brazil's most celebrated novelists despite limited formal education. Beginning his career as a typesetter and journalist, he went on to write psychologically incisive fiction that transformed Brazilian literature. As the founding president of the Brazilian Academy of Letters, he helped cement Rio's status as a literary capital.

El Ateneo Grand Splendid

Buenos Aires

ARGENTINA | SOUTH AMERICA

Forged by migration and social upheaval, the Argentinian capital is an intricate web of stories—some, like the country's famed music, are melancholic; others defy definition altogether.

Buenos Aires has rarely been stagnant. Over the centuries, this bustling port city has been shaped by waves of immigration, with folks flocking here from all over the world in search of a better life. Years of boom and bust have rolled in like a river mist, while new languages and styles have been woven together to create a cultural tapestry that is truly unique. True, it's not been easy—what with multiple coups and dictatorships—but it's only served as a pressure cooker for fierce imaginative resistance and seriously inventive literary forms. This all came to the fore in the 20th century, when local legend Jorge Luis Borges toyed with magical realism, breaking the boundaries of fantasy and philosophy, and bushy-browed Julio Cortázar turned the streets into a showground for surreal play. There's still something surreal about the city's output today—just look at Mariana Enriquez's Neo-Gothic tales.

The Porteños (the locals) keep these literary fires burning strong. Places that celebrate the city's bookish heritage remain at the heart of Buenos Aires, with museums going the extra mile to preserve local literature and world-class bookstores remaining fiercely independent. It's safe to say that Argentina's passion for good books remains as strong as ever.

GETTING AROUND

The city center is easily manageable on foot or by bike. While public transit can also get you far, schoolbook Spanish might not: here, the metro is known as the *subte* and buses are *colectivos* or *bondis*.

READING LIST

The Slaughter Yard

Esteban Echeverría

Set in a Buenos Aires abattoir, this short story depicts a single day in 1839 and the violence that ensues from the brutal Argentinian regime.

Our Share of Night

Mariana Enriquez

Written by contemporary journalist and novelist Mariana Enriquez, this Gothic horror takes place in the aftermath of Argentina's military dictatorship—expect a good deal of body horror and the supernatural.

The Kiss of the Spider Woman

Manuel Puig

Two cellmates—Valentin, a hardened revolutionary, and Molina, a histrionic gay man—form an unlikely bond in this 1970s masterpiece by LGBTQ+ activist and writer Manuel Puig.

London City

As you step through the doors of this historic café, you'll be greeted by a rather quirky-looking wooden statue. With his thick-rimmed glasses, Cuban cigar, and characteristic bushy unibrow, he is—at least for those in the know—unmistakably Julio Cortázar, one of Argentina's greatest writers. It was here, back in the 1950s, that the author sat down to write his first novel, *The Winners*, and even set part of it within these walls. If the Cortázar carving could talk, he'd tell you that "La London" (as locals know it) hasn't changed an awful lot since his glory days. It's still all checkerboard floors, chandeliers, and marble surfaces. So, even today as you sip your coffee and munch on a *medialuna* (croissants, in Argentina), you can imagine Cortázar sitting right next to you, scribbling away.

☞ Avenida de Mayo 599, Montserrat; londoncity.com.ar

Café Tortoni

Librería de Ávila

Librería de Ávila holds the title of being the longest-standing bookshop not just in Buenos Aires, but on the entire continent ... as long as you ignore a brief hiatus in the 1980s. Just a stone's throw from the famed Casa Rosada presidential palace (the one with Eva Perón's famous balcony, as seen in *Evita*), this print emporium once stocked the libraries of Spanish colonial administrators. Later, the *libertadores* and founding fathers of the country would flock here to stock up on imported French titles, to spur on their dreams of independence. Though it was once at risk of being bought out by a burger chain (shivers), Librería de Ávila has prevailed and remains true to its historical prestige. Wander in past its rusty shutters and aging signs and you'll find a veritable treasure trove of ancient manuscripts, dusty tomes, and rare books. There are more recent publications on offer too, but really, you're here for the history.

☞ Calle de Adolfo Alsina 500, Montserrat

Café Tortoni

When you fix your eyes on Café Tortoni, you'll see why Buenos Aires is known as the "Paris of the South." The Art Nouveau entrance, the stained-glass ceiling, the marble surfaces: everything hints at the café's French origins (it was opened in 1858 by a Frenchman known as Touan). Tortoni's charms were not lost on the city's artists and writers, who gathered here for coffee and even started their own culture club, La Peña del Tortoni, in the 1920s, though they were relegated to the basement (space has always come at a premium here, so expect a line, even to this day). You can still catch poet Alfonsina Storni and literary titan Borges holding court here, albeit in the form of slightly bizarre statues. Why not join them for a *café con leche*?

☞ Avenida de Mayo 825, Montserrat; cafetortoni.com.ar

Biblioteca Nacional de Maestros

Biblioteca Nacional de Maestros

A few days in Buenos Aires is enough to know that its best-kept gems are often hiding in plain sight. Take the National Library of Teachers, located in the hulking, eclectically decorated Pizzurno Palace—which sticks out like a sore thumb just off one of the city's main boulevards. Most tourists don't go inside, but those in on the secret are treated to gorgeous reading rooms with old wood panels and elegant green columns. The site was originally founded as a resource for education professionals, but today it provides an oasis for teachers, students, and bookworms alike.

Pasaje de Pizzurno 953, Recoleta; bnm.me.gov.ar

Eterna Cadencia

Dark-wood shelves, wrought-iron chandeliers, and overflowing piles of books: it's hard to believe that this bookstore has only been operating for 20 years. (Of course, the 19th-century townhouse that hosts it has been around much longer.) Despite the old-school charm, modernity makes its mark in the atrium café, bedecked with hanging plants. It's here, and up on the glorious roof terrace, where the hip literati of Palermo Hollywood (Buenos Aires's chicest barrio) get together to sip Malbec, discuss the latest Mariana Enriquez novel, or cheer on their friend's book launch.

Calle Honduras 5582, Palermo; eternacadencia.com.ar

Fundación Borges

You just can't talk about 20th-century literature without mentioning Borges. The Buenos Aires bard's essays and short stories put Argentina on the map and reshaped world literature through his chimerical blend of philosophy and myth-making. The Borges Foundation, established by his widow and literary executrix, María Kodama, now preserves and promotes his labyrinthine legacy, running regular talks on his work and influence. A little secret: the foundation is actually the house next door to the writer's former home, but its museum does contain a re-creation of Borges's bedroom. Fans can also feast their eyes on a large section of the library that inspired many of his *Ficciones* (short stories) and some of the author's personal effects, which are displayed alongside manuscripts, first editions, and personal photographs.

☞ Calle de Dr. Tomás Manuel de Anchorena 1660, Recoleta; fundacionborges.com.ar

Biblioteca Nacional Mariano Moreno

Argentina's national library—with its Brutalist blocks, concrete corners and hovering halls—feels like a spaceship has crash landed in the city. The building may be undeniably modern, but the institution itself is as old as Argentina. Established in 1810 by founding father Mariano Moreno, the library was a means to educate the nation and breathe some culture back into civil life long stifled by the Spanish Empire. And it took its role seriously—just look through the collections: part of the first Gutenberg Bible, the largest media archive in Latin America, unpublished Alejandra Pizarnik manuscripts (an Argentinian poet), the list goes on. Come to study, read, or simply linger in the reading rooms, which overlook the Río de la Plata estuary.

☞ Calle Agüero 2502, Recoleta; bn.gov.ar

El Ateneo Grand Splendid

If bookstores had a beauty contest, this one might win the prize. Housed in the former Grand Splendid Theater—and that name is by no means a misnomer—El Ateneo turns literature into a true spectacle. Under an impressive frescoed dome, the stalls and circles where audiences once sat now feature rows upon rows of tomes on every subject under the sun. As well as being one of the most beautiful, this is also one of the largest bookstores in the world. After rifling through the shelves, and taking your fair share of photographs, head to one of the reading nooks in the former box seats to make the most of the views. Or take to the stage, which is now home to a café framed by red velvet curtains; here, patrons peruse their latest finds and engage in bookish banter over strong coffee.

☞ Avenida de Santa Fe 1860, Recoleta; yenny-elateneo.com

Villa Ocampo

Out in the leafy suburb of Béccar lies Villa Ocampo, the majestic stately home of Victoria Ocampo, a true cultural trailblazer: her magazine, *Sur*, helped to connect Latin American writers with broader literary trends around the world and she frequently hosted literary gatherings. Visit this pristinely preserved mansion and you'll be following in the footsteps of literary titans like Albert Camus, Graham Greene, and Antoine de Saint-Exupéry. The most frequent visitors, however, were Victoria's sister, Silvina Ocampo, and brother-in-law, Adolfo Bioy Casares, two of the precursors to magical realism in Argentina. If you want to pay your respects, head back into the city center to Recoleta Cemetery, where the three of them now rest, alongside other big names of Argentinian culture.

☞ Calle de Elortondo 1837, Béccar; asociacionamigosdevillaocampo.org.ar

Biblioteca Nacional Mariano Moreno

Daunt Books

London

ENGLAND, UK | EUROPE

When it comes to literary history, few cities rival London. The UK's capital has been a center of writing for centuries, nurturing world-famous wordsmiths (Shakespeare, Dickens, Woolf) and continually celebrating their legacy.

London's cast of literary characters could fill all 775 rooms of Buckingham Palace. There's Charles Dickens's plucky Pip, Arthur Conan Doyle's uber-observant Sherlock Holmes, Michael Bond's marmalade-loving Paddington Bear, and Helen Fielding's all-too-relatable Bridget Jones—the list goes on. The UK's capital appears as a setting in more books than any other European city, and just as many of our favorite protagonists are based in London, so were many of their creators.

Way back in the 16th century, William Shakespeare was writing and performing his plays to the masses by the Thames River. As the city expanded in the 18th and 19th centuries, more creative minds moved in (including Dickens). Then came the Modernists (Virginia Woolf and the nonconformist Bloomsbury Group; *p.87*), followed by a slew of seminal contemporary writers, such as Sam Selvon and Zadie Smith.

But London doesn't just write; it publishes and it sells. Most publishing houses have a base here, and come spring, you'll find them talking shop at the bustling London Book Fair. Bookstores, meanwhile, come in all shapes and sizes. There are big ones, small ones, dedicated spaces for the LGBTQ+ community, the romance lovers, the political rebels. The Big Smoke has it all.

GETTING AROUND

London is walkable, to a point. While many of the city's landmarks are centrally located, this sprawling, centuries-old city is huge, so expect to hop on the Underground (Tube) or bus from time to time.

READING LIST

Bleak House

Charles Dickens

Bleak House may be a beast of a book (nearly 1,000 pages), but this multigenerational tale of a seemingly endless lawsuit is a Victorian masterpiece and, some say, Dickens's best novel.

The Lonely Londoners

Sam Selvon

Giving voice to the Windrush generation, Selvon's account of the harsh realities of Trinidadians who migrated to the city in the 1950s is a vital piece of London literature.

White Teeth

Zadie Smith

Exploring themes of multiculturalism and identity, Zadie Smith's dazzling debut tells the story of an unlikely friendship between two veterans and their families living in North London.

New Beacon Books

Set up in 1966 by John La Rose and his partner, Sarah White, New Beacon Books was the UK's first Black publisher and bookstore. It's played a pivotal role in its community, promoting African and Caribbean voices through its publishing arm and celebrating them with an exciting calendar of book launches, reading salons, and children's story-time sessions. It's a place worth treasuring—and locals would certainly agree. In 2017 and then again in 2021, the community rallied behind New Beacon Books, raising funds to save the shop from closure.

76 Stroud Green Road, Finsbury Park; newbeaconbooks.com

Shakespeare's Globe

John Sandoe Books

London's Chelsea neighborhood is a lovely place to wander, its leafy streets dotted with boutique shops and photogenic cafés. It's also where you'll find one of London's most picturesque bookstores. Sprawled across three 18th-century buildings, John Sandoe Books is crammed with good books. They're piled on old-fashioned tables, stacked on stairs, and hidden away on secret sliding shelves—meaning you'll discover something new every time you visit.

10–12 Blacklands Terrace, Chelsea; johnsandoe.com

Shakespeare's Globe

English literature and language wouldn't be the same without Shakespeare. The world-renowned Bard wrote some 37 plays and 154 sonnets, works that inspired countless writers after him. Many of those plays were first performed here, at the Globe Theatre, or at least at the old one (which burned down centuries ago). The version that stands here now is a thrilling reconstruction. It's an open-air, O-shaped space, where actors project over the sound of the city (these

LITERARY FESTIVAL

London Literature Festival

This annual takeover of the city's Southbank Centre welcomes literary folk from around the world for author talks, poetry readings, and family-friendly sessions. It usually takes place in October *(southbankcenter.co.uk)*.

days, mainly passing airplanes) and groundlings (the standing audience) watch come rain or shine.

21 New Globe Walk, Bankside; shakespearesglobe.com

Cecil Court

London wears much of its history on its sleeve—landmarks like the Tower of London and St. Paul's Cathedral still loom on the ever-growing skyline—but there are plenty of treasures hidden at ground level, too. Take Cecil Court. This quaint alleyway is lined with some two dozen antique and secondhand bookstores. But it wasn't always so. Established in the 17th century, Cecil Court was first home to a motley crew of traders (brothels, barbers, and blacksmiths); it later welcomed Wolfgang Amadeus Mozart, who lived here while touring in 1764; then in the Edwardian era, it became Flicker Alley, the hub of the British film industry. Finally, in the 1930s, the booksellers moved in, and they've been here ever since.

Covent Garden; cecilcourt.co.uk

Ye Olde Cheshire Cheese

Meeting friends at Ye Olde Cheshire Cheese isn't always straightforward. This age-old watering hole is a dimly lit warren of rooms spread across multiple floors; even its entrance, squirreled away down an alleyway, isn't easy to find. It's hardly changed since it was rebuilt after the Great Fire of London in 1666, so it's easy to picture past regulars stumbling across the old floorboards, beer sloshing in hand, searching for their friends. And they weren't your usual regulars. Writers Mark Twain and Charles Dickens frequented this spot. Perhaps the most iconic, however, was Polly. This African gray parrot lived in the bar and became famous for its foul mouth—so famous that Polly's death in 1926 featured in global newspapers.

145 Fleet St., City of London; ye-olde-cheshire-cheese.co.uk

Cecil Court

Waterstones Piccadilly

You'll find Waterstones bookstores across the UK, but none compare to the Piccadilly branch. Featuring 8 miles (13 km) of bookshelves, this is the largest bookstore not just in the UK, but in the whole of Europe. It's spread over a whopping eight floors, all dotted with Art Deco touches (the building dates from the 1930s). Titles cover every subject imaginable, and there's also an assortment of games, vinyl records, and souvenirs. After losing an hour (or three) here, head down the road to nearby Hatchards. Founded in 1797, it's the oldest bookstore in the UK and its five floors are packed with plenty of charm.

203–206 Piccadilly, Piccadilly; waterstones.com

British Library

Can't find what you're looking for in the city's many bookstores? Head to the British Library instead. Home to some 170 million items (including nearly every printed book in the UK), the country's national library is like a Hogwarts banquet for literary lovers. Researchers from all around the world flock here to see the building's many treasures (which include the second-largest atlas in the world and two of the surviving Magna Carta documents), but this is more than just a literary repository. Entrepreneurial locals gather for free business classes, families drop by for the creative children's sessions, and students and freelancers tap away on laptops in one of the 11 grand reading rooms. Be sure to get a free Reader's Pass in advance if you want to access the collection and the reading rooms.

☞ 96 Euston Road, King's Cross; bl.uk

Charles Dickens Museum

Beloved British author Charles Dickens lived in various places around London, but this 19th-century terraced house is the only one remaining. Fortunately, it's also one of the most important. Dickens was hugely productive while living here, scribbling away at novels including *Oliver Twist* and *Nicholas Nickleby*. Those rooms in which he lived and wrote have since been transformed into this fascinating museum, with furniture arranged just as it was during the writer's era. Exhibits fill the space—there are personal effects like old letters, old playbills, and a snuff box, plus some first editions of his famous works. Once you've taken it all in, head for tea and cake at the museum's on-site café, the Artful Tea Room (named after a certain quick-fingered thief from *Oliver Twist*).

☞ 48–49 Doughty Street, Bloomsbury; dickensmuseum.com

Gay's the Word

Community always comes first at Gay's the Word. Founded in 1979 by a group of gay socialists, this is now the UK's oldest LGBTQ+ bookshop. It's packed with queer history books, love stories, and literary fiction, but it hasn't survived for so long simply because of the books. Gay's the Word has long been a safe space for its community, its walls lined with rainbow flags and colorful posters, and its staff among the most welcoming in the business. It also offers a range of inclusive book clubs, and community meetups and discussion groups for LGBTQ+ folks. Meanwhile, its website serves as an important information resource, with a host of advice for LGBTQ+ folk, plus parents and teachers. This place is activism and inclusivity done right; as a result, it's a stalwart of London's literary scene.

☞ 66 Marchmont Street, Bloomsbury; gaystheword.co.uk

Daunt Books

Take a walk around London and you'll inevitably spot someone with a Daunt Books tote bag. Loved by locals, this iconic bookstore was founded on Marylebone High Street in 1990, though you'd think it much older. It's set within an old Edwardian building and famed for its gorgeous oak gallery, complete with huge skylights, elegant dark-wood bookcases, and a stunning stained-glass window. Initially specializing in travel books, it's since expanded to cover most genres, but the gallery area is still dedicated to books arranged by country—perfect for those looking for a themed holiday read. Buy enough books (usually around £40 worth) and you'll get a free cotton tote bag; the enviable colored one doesn't come for free, though.

☞ 84 Marylebone High Street, Marylebone; dauntbooks.co.uk

British Library

Word on the Water

Word on the Water

Want to stand out in London's crowded bookstore market? Why not build a bookstore on a boat? So thought Word on the Water. The so-called London Bookbarge began life as a migratory bookstore, before it was granted a permanent mooring on Regent's Canal Towpath in 2015. Since then, the owners have filled every nook and cranny of this old Dutch barge with books, and even hosted poetry readings and musical performances on its roof. It's quirky London at its very best, and locals can't get enough: join them cycling along the canal and pausing to snap some photographs in the sun, before descending below deck to browse the eclectic stock.

Regent's Canal Towpath, King's Cross; wordonthewater.co.uk

Keats House

One of many author homes in this literary city, Keats House is set in the lovely North London neighborhood of Hampstead. John Keats lived here for just two years, but it was a prime time in the Romantic poet's life. He fell in love with his neighbor Fanny Brawne and wrote some of his most famous poems in the house, including favorites like "La Belle Dame sans Merci" and "Ode to the Nightingale." His gorgeous Regency villa has been well preserved and now operates as both a museum (featuring mementos of the poet's life) and literary center. The best way to explore is on a tour (included in the admission price), which operate on Thursday, Friday, and Sunday afternoons.

10 Keats Grove, Hampstead; keatsfoundation.com

Bloomsbury Group

This leafy corner of North London became famous in the early 1900s for its association with a particularly bookish circle of friends. The forward-thinking Bloomsbury Group gathered in the elegant townhouses here and changed London's literary landscape forever.

DISTANCE
2 miles (3 km)

WALKING TIME
Allow an hour

NEAREST TRANSIT
Euston Tube station is ideally located at the start and end of the route

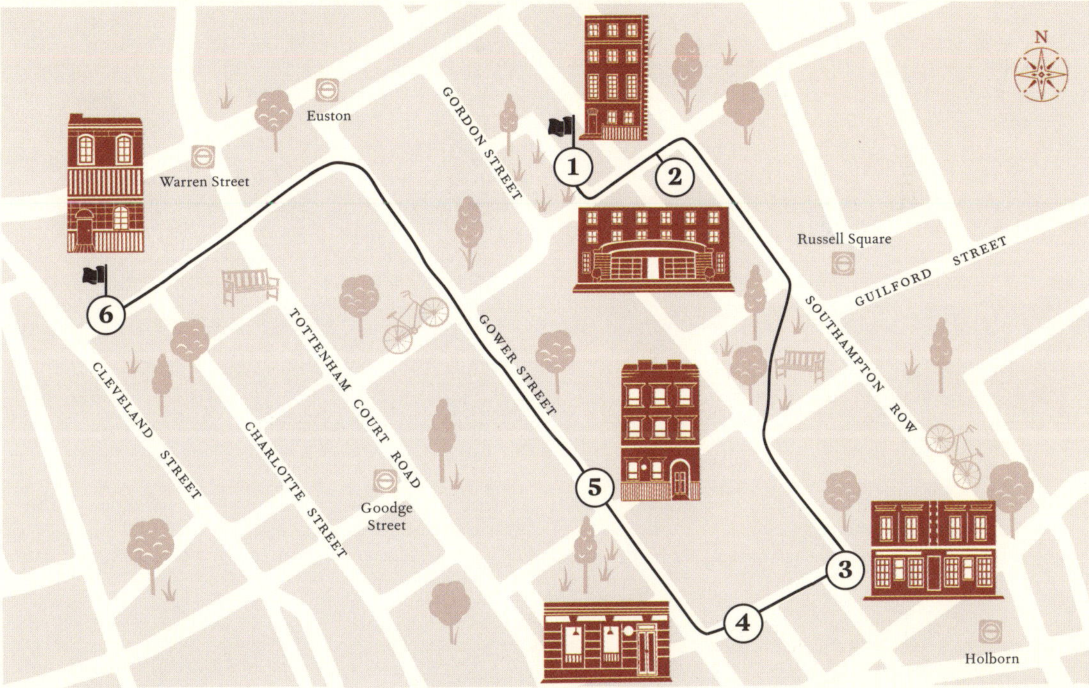

1. 46 Gordon Square

The beginnings of the Bloomsbury Group can be traced back to this address, where Virginia Woolf and her sister Vanessa Bell hosted the group's famous Thursday evening gatherings.

2. Tavistock Hotel

The Tavistock Hotel marks the site of Woolf's home between 1924 and 1939; she wrote two of her most famous novels here, *To the Lighthouse* and *Mrs. Dalloway (48–55 Tavistock Sq).*

3. London Review Bookshop

Arguably the area's most famous bookstore, the London Review Bookshop is a haven for contemporary intellects; it's run by the eponymous literary magazine *(14–16 Bury Pl).*

4. Jarndyce Booksellers

Another beloved bookstore, Jarndyce specializes in rare books from the 17th, 18th, and 19th centuries. It's a gorgeous little time capsule inside and out *(46 Great Russell St.).*

5. 10 Gower Street

Thought to be the inspiration for D. H. Lawrence's Lady Chatterley, aristocrat Lady Ottoline Morrell regularly hosted gatherings for writers (including Woolf and T. S. Eliot) at her home.

6. 29 Fitzroy Square

Woolf later moved here, the former home of George Bernard Shaw. The Thursday gatherings continued, though rumor has it they became more physical and less conversational.

Oxford, the City of Dreaming Spires

Oxford

ENGLAND, UK | EUROPE

Weird and wonderful worlds have been dreamed up in Oxford. This beloved university city has long been the realm of fantasy writers who (lucky for us) let their imaginations run wild among its scenic streets and cozy pubs.

There's something about Oxford. Whether it's the city's age-old academic heritage, its swoon-worthy limestone buildings, or its array of independent shops, the City of Dreaming Spires is, undeniably, rather magical. And some of the world's greatest fantasy writers would certainly agree.

It was here that J. R. R. Tolkien created his elves, ents, and evil lords for *The Lord of the Rings*. And where C. S. Lewis wrote about four children who walked through a wardrobe and into the world of Narnia. Philip Pullman also drew inspiration from his time in Oxford to craft Lyra's school in *His Dark Materials*. So too did Lewis Carroll, who came up with the curious tale of *Alice's Adventures in Wonderland* here. And that's not forgetting the numerous scenes from the *Harry Potter* film series that were shot in and around the university.

That famed university has been here since 1096, making it one of the oldest in the world. Over the centuries, students have flooded its halls—including many of those famed writers, who studied and taught here—and bookstores, student bars, and libraries promptly followed. Much of the city is still catered toward the university, so expect bookstores packed with academic texts, alongside those beloved fantasy tomes.

GETTING AROUND

Walking around Oxford is a breeze—distances between key attractions are short and streets are scenic. To move between sights even quicker, consider renting a bike (like many of the students here).

READING LIST

Brideshead Revisited

Evelyn Waugh

Charles Ryder befriends the wealthy Flyte family, navigating romance, family dynamics, and the complexities of life in England's interwar upper class.

Northern Lights

Philip Pullman

Philip Pullman's epic tale of Dust, daemons, and a dark, mysterious world begins with Lyra uncovering secrets in a fictional Oxford college named Jordan College.

The Lord of the Rings

J. R. R. Tolkien

J. R. R. Tolkien's legendary saga of Frodo the hobbit, the One Ring, and the fate of Middle-Earth was largely dreamed up while he wandered Oxford's streets and colleges.

The Bodleian's Radcliffe Camera

The Bodleian

Oh, the Bodleian! With its domed reading rooms, elaborate Gothic ceilings, and bookshelves packed with rare books, this university library is easily one of the UK's best. It was founded in 1602 (it's one of the oldest libraries in Europe) and now hosts some 13 million printed items across its many shelves. But it's not just one building. The Bodleian is actually a network of 23 libraries, with its central core—the Old Bodleian Library, Duke Humfrey's Library, Radcliffe Camera, and the Divinity School—promising the most beautiful rooms. Walking around these historic buildings feels like stepping back in time, or stepping into another world (both the Divinity School and Duke Humfrey's Library appear in *Harry Potter*, as Hogwarts's infirmary and student library respectively). Note that the only way you can explore these buildings is via a guided tour—book an evening tour for the most atmospheric adventure (no invisibility cloak required).

☞ Broad Street, City Center; bodleian.ox.ac.uk

Gulp Fiction

Oxford is packed with historical literary landmarks, but there are a few new kids on the block, too. Take Gulp Fiction, a bookstore-bar hidden away in Oxford's Covered Market. Founded by book lover and former Blackwell's bookseller Oliver Mason, this indie bookstore offers a curated collection of titles—ranging from travel writing to literary fiction—but that's not all. Drop by for one of Gulp Fiction's buzzy literary meet-ups: a book club, a writing group, or an author event perhaps. Alternatively, you could sign up for a Book Lovers' Happy Hour session—you'll be offered well-thought-out book recommendations from the staff here, alongside delicious, personalized cocktails. Cheers to that.

☞ Unit 28, 29 Covered Market, City Center; gulpfictionbooks.com

The Eagle and Child

"This, my friend, is a pint," said Merry the hobbit, and so, perhaps, said Tolkien. The author frequented this age-old pub in the 1930s and 1940s, along with C. S. Lewis and other members of the Inklings, a literary discussion group. Under the dim lights, they read their work together, sparking ideas for their fantasy epics. The pub has been undergoing renovations since 2020, with plans to reopen in 2027 with minimal changes to the interior (hopefully those ghosts of the literary past will remain). If it's not open yet, you can still get your Tolkien fix a 25-minute walk away. His Oxford home (a private residence with a memorial plaque) is at 20 Northmoor Road; it was here that he wrote *The Hobbit* and most of *The Lord of the Rings*.

☞ 49 St. Giles', City Center

The Kilns

You may not be able to enter Tolkien's Oxford residence, but you can visit the home of his friend and fellow fantasy writer, C. S. Lewis. Known as the Kilns, this quaint cottage was the home of Lewis from 1930 until his death in 1963. He wrote all seven *Narnia* books while teaching at Oxford and, later, Cambridge. To visit the property, you'll need to book a tour in advance, because the house is actually a study center rather than a museum (a select group of scholars live and work here). But don't let this lived-in aspect put you off; passionate tour guides promise a tour packed with tales of Lewis (also known as Jack), his family, friends, and his beloved books. Afterward, be sure to walk down to nearby Holy Trinity Church, where Lewis once worshipped and is now buried—a stained-glass window in the church shows scenes from the world of Narnia (spot Aslan, the Dawn Treader, and Cair Paravel).

Lewis Close, Headington; cslewis.org

AUTHOR PROFILE

J. R. R. Tolkien

The father of modern fantasy crafted worlds rich in characters, invented several languages and wrote dense mythologies (see *The Silmarillion*). He grew up around Birmingham, studied at Exeter College, Oxford, and, soon after, served during World War I. After the war and a stint at the University of Leeds, he settled again in Oxford, teaching English and writing "to the end of his days."

Blackwell's

Every Oxford student knows Blackwell's. With its iconic blue façade, this university bookstore has stood guard over Broad Street since 1879. Over the decades, it's seen the city transform around it: cobbled Broad Street became paved, horses became cars, and more and more students passed through its doors, their empty tote bags ready to be filled with books. And, inevitably, Blackwell's has changed, too. As demand has grown, the bookstore has expanded, opening new rooms, adding a basement floor, and opening more branches around the UK (but the Broad Street branch is the best). Whether you're looking for an obscure book of essays, a little-known novel, or a forgotten philosophical text, this academic haven will probably have it.

48-51 Broad Street, City Center; blackwells.co.uk

Blackwell's

Addyman Books

Hay-on-Wye

WALES, UK | EUROPE

Despite being home to just 2,000 residents, Hay-on-Wye is packed with bookish brilliance. Tucked amid velvety green, sheep-dotted fields, the Welsh border town is famed for being the world's first "book town," thanks to the abundance of bookstores dotting its winding streets. But that's not all: this well-read spot also hosts the Hay Festival, one of the world's most celebrated literary events.

Richard Booth's Books

Housed in a refurbished agricultural hall, this three-level treasure trove was Richard Booth's pride and joy. Its handmade wooden shelves are crammed with new and secondhand books.

boothbooks.co.uk

Gay on Wye

Located behind a cute, candy-pink façade, this warm and welcoming bookstore is all about LGBTQ+ reads.

gayonwye.com

The Poetry Bookshop

Founded in 1979 by Christopher and Melanie Prince, this spot has the UK's most extensive collection of poetry.

poetrybookshop.co.uk

Murder and Mayhem

Crime and horror titles fill the shelves of this little bookstore, whose kooky decor includes a fake tombstone and a chalk outline of a man on the floor.

5 Lion Street

Honesty Bookshop

This al fresco bookstore is a charming spot in Hay Castle's old moat. To purchase something, simply pop a pound in the honesty box.

Castle Street

It's largely due to Richard Booth that Hay earned its "book town" moniker. In 1962, this eccentric literature lover opened a secondhand bookstore here; over the next decade, other booksellers followed Booth's lead, setting up shop in Hay. It wasn't until April 1, 1977, though, that Hay found global fame, after Booth declared the town an independent nation and crowned himself King Richard the Bookheart (his horse, Goldie, was declared prime minister). The unconventional move drummed up plenty of press and placed Hay firmly on the map as a literary destination; by the 1980s there were over 30 bookstores.

Around 20 remain, and they're at their busiest during the Hay Festival. Established in 1988 (in a pub garden), this annual event—the UK's largest literary festival—now welcomes tens of thousands of book lovers.

Richard Booth

Bath Old Books

Bath

ENGLAND, UK | EUROPE

Bath belongs to Jane Austen. The iconic author lived in this Georgian city for five years, and some of her beloved novels were inspired by her time here. This literary history lives on today in Jane-themed events and a host of unique bookstores.

Regency romance, fancy balls, woeful suitors: welcome to Georgian Bath, home of Jane Austen. Ever since the author moved here from her childhood home in Hampshire in 1801, this Somerset city has been more than a little obsessed with her, and for good reason. Austen spent five years in Bath, finding herself (as a gentleman's daughter) at the heart of fashionable society; inspired by her new home (today, Britain's only UNESCO World Heritage City) and its gossiping gentry class, she wrote two Bath-based novels, *Northanger Abbey* and *Persuasion*. That was some centuries ago, but Austen's work remains adored worldwide, and Bath hasn't changed much since she left. The cobblestone streets and Georgian buildings still stand—as do the far older Roman Baths, which give the Spa City its moniker—so Bath today isn't so different from Bath in Austen's era. No wonder the TV series *Bridgerton*, a Regency romp based on author Julia Quinn's books, was shot in the city.

What's beyond the silks and scandals? Well, Mary Shelley wrote much of *Frankenstein* while in Bath, and Charles Dickens satirized its social life in *The Pickwick Papers*. What's more, Bath has tons of bookstores packed with local literature—if your one true love is books, you're sure to find a match here.

GETTING AROUND

Diminutive Bath is easily walkable, though be mindful of all those cobblestone streets. Driving through the center can be tricky; instead, consider using the Park and Ride shuttle service.

READING LIST

Persuasion

Jane Austen

Anne Elliot faces a second chance at romance when her past lover reappears in her life. But there's plenty more to Austen's Bath-based novel than romance.

Islands of Mercy

Rose Tremain

Set in Victorian Bath and far-off Borneo, *Islands of Mercy* follows intertwined characters as they search for freedom, identity, and moral purpose.

Frankenstein

Mary Shelley

While the story spans multiple locations, Bath serves as a key backdrop in this Gothic classic, grounding Victor Frankenstein's social and scientific circles.

The Jane Austen Centre

Love all things Austen? Look no further. The Jane Austen Centre offers a comprehensive look at the life and works of Bath's most famous literary figure. Appropriately set in a Georgian townhouse—just a short walk from Austen's former Bath residence, 25 Gay Street—the center features a host of literary exhibitions, including a lifelike waxwork of the author and a costume room where fans can dress up in Regency-era clothes. Visits all begin with an introductory talk (conducted by knowledgeable, costumed, and ever-enthusiastic staff), after which you're welcome to explore on your own. The center is also home to the beloved Regency Tea Room, where afternoon tea is served under the prideful gaze of Mr. Darcy (here, in his incomparable Colin Firth iteration).

☞ 40 Gay Street, City Centre; janeausten.co.uk

Mr B's Emporium of Reading Delights

Bath has plenty of charming bookstores, but Mr B's might be its most loved. Why? Because this uber-friendly bookstore takes customer service to a whole new level. Handwritten recommendations from staff line the bookshelves, a colorful and welcoming children's corner entices young readers, and the shop also offers a custom reading subscription service and, better yet, so-called Reading Spas. The latter involves a chat with a passionate bookseller about your favorite genres (accompanied by coffee and cake, of course); the bookseller will then curate a pile of personalized books for you to take home. It's bibliotherapy at its very best, and it's so popular that you'll need to book a session months in advance.

☞ 13–15 John Street, City Centre; mrbsemporium.com

Topping & Company Booksellers

Set within a grand Grade II–listed building, Topping & Company's Bath branch—there's another great one in Edinburgh *(p. 103)*—is the stuff of any book lover's dreams. Pass through the lofty entrance columns and you'll enter the vast central hall, decorated with ornate picture rails, nifty ladders to reach the highest shelves, and, surprise, surprise, lots and lots of books. An elegant staircase connects two of the floors, while a basement offers plenty more room for the shop's encyclopedic literary collection; there's also a selection of rare editions on display. To sweeten the deal, Topping & Co offers complimentary tea and coffee, which you can enjoy at one of the tables dotted around the shop, along with your new purchase.

☞ York Street, City Centre; toppingbooks.co.uk

Bath Old Books

Is this Bath's best secondhand bookstore? It's certainly the city's most charming. Located in a quaint townhouse just around the corner from the Royal Crescent (a masterclass in Georgian architecture and one of Bath's most beautiful areas), Bath Old Books comprises two floors, filled floor-to-ceiling with secondhand books. Helpful staff will guide you to specific titles or genres, or you can simply roam the quaint rooms yourself—you might stumble across an old Jane Austen edition, a gorgeous vintage title, or a rare forgotten masterpiece that's just waiting to be loved again. There are some real treasures in this lovely little shop, if you take the time to find them.

☞ 9C Margaret's Buildings, City Centre; 01225 422244

Persephone Books

Persephone Books

In a city dominated by two female writers—Austen and Shelley—Persephone Books fits right in. This independent publisher reprints neglected literary works by (largely) female writers, most dating from the mid-20th century. Books are wrapped in elegant, gray dust jackets, complete with colorful endpapers (designs of which are chosen to reflect the era of the book), and placed proudly on the shelves. Dotted with fresh flowers and vintage posters, this sunny bookstore is perfect for present-buying—especially for that friend who seems to have read everything.

8 Edgar Buildings, City Centre; persephonebooks.co.uk

LITERARY FESTIVAL

Jane Austen Festival

This annual 10-day event kicks off in September with the famous Regency Costumed Promenade, where hundreds of people waltz down the streets in Austen-era garb. Balls, tours, and theatrical performances follow, all in the name of Jane.

The West Yorkshire moors

Brontë Country

ENGLAND, UK | EUROPE

Amid the rolling moors and gray-stone buildings of West Yorkshire, three sisters quietly changed the English literary canon forever. Whether you know the Brontës from the wind-swept world of Wuthering Heights *or the fierce heroines of* Jane Eyre *and* The Tenant of Wildfell Hall, *the northerly English region in which Charlotte, Emily, and Anne lived is on every bookish traveler's bucket list.*

Brontë Parsonage Museum

The sisters spent most of their lives in this Haworth house and wrote their acclaimed novels here. Visitors can gaze upon original furniture, old letters, and clothing items.

bronte.org.uk

Old School Room

Just down the road from the museum is the Old School Room, where the Brontës once taught classes. Along the same road is St. Michael and All Angels Church graveyard, where you'll find the Brontë family tomb.

hawortholdschoolroom.org.uk

Main Street

Haworth's cobbled Main Street is also a highlight: it's lined with lovely shops and cozy pubs, and, perhaps best of all, promises views of the moors Emily was so fascinated by.

Top Withens

A short walk out of town leads you straight to the moors. Don't miss Top Withens (thought to have inspired the *Wuthering Heights* farmhouse ruins) and Brontë Waterfall (beloved by the sisters). But really, you're simply here to ramble and roam, just as Cathy did in Emily's imagination.

Few literary icons are as inextricably linked to the land as the Brontës are to West Yorkshire. Think of their work and you'll undoubtedly picture the moors that surround their hometown and dominate Emily's famed novel, *Wuthering Heights*. The sisters, and their work, were born from this rugged, remote land, and it remains little changed today: hills are still blanketed in purple heather, the wind is ever-present, and a sense of isolation prevails—perhaps the land heard Cathy's call to "make the moors never change and you and I never change."

Most trips to this lonely landscape begin in Haworth, the Brontë family's hometown. The sisters lived much of their short lives in this poor Yorkshire village. It's come a long way since the mid-19th century (all cute shops and cafés), but much of the Brontës' history remains.

Brontë sisters

Makars' Court

Edinburgh

SCOTLAND, UK | EUROPE

With its brooding castle, cobbled streets, and rich history, Edinburgh is a city that ignites the imagination. Writers old and new have long been drawn to the Scottish capital, and so too have book lovers keen to explore its literary heritage.

Edinburgh's literary pedigree is uncontested, with the city claiming a clutch of bookish firsts. This was where the first book in Scotland was printed in 1508; where the world's first circulating library opened in 1725; and where, in 1760, the first-ever English department was established. No wonder the city was named UNESCO's inaugural City of Literature in 2004. Edinburgh also counts many famous writers among its locals, from famed 19th-century novelist Sir Walter Scott to one of the 20th century's most celebrated writers, Muriel Spark. The city has birthed a cast of unforgettable characters, too: the Janus-faced Dr. Jekyll and Mr. Hyde were born amid the winding wynds of the Old Town, while razor-sharp detective Sherlock Holmes came to life in the hallowed halls of the city's medical school.

With such heritage, Edinburgh could easily rest on its literary laurels, but it doesn't. This is a city that actively encourages the creation and celebration of writing, especially at the annual Edinburgh International Book Festival, which puts on more than 700 events. And year-round? Well, there are monuments and museums dedicated to famous writers, and countless libraries and cozy bookstores—all waiting to be discovered.

GETTING AROUND

Edinburgh is a very walkable city with a compact city center. There's also a comprehensive bus network and a tram line. Driving is not recommended, due to congestion and limited parking.

READING LIST

The Heart of Midlothian

Sir Walter Scott

Scott's prolific output made him a master of historical novels, and this is one of his best. Expect themes of justice, family, and religious piety.

The Prime of Miss Jean Brodie

Muriel Spark

Set in a girls' school in the 1930s, *The Prime of Miss Jean Brodie* focuses on an eccentric schoolmistress who teaches her students unconventional, romantic ideals. It's short, scintillating, and spirited (or rather, Sparky ...).

44 Scotland Street

Alexander McCall Smith

The first installment (of 17 books, as of 2026) of the contemporary *44 Scotland Street* series has a colorful cast of characters, who live in a single New Town building.

Writers' Museum

Writers' Museum and Makars' Court

Tucked away in a turreted 17th-century building, this intimate museum honors three greats of Scottish literature: bard Robert Burns, novelist and poet Sir Walter Scott, and writer Robert Louis Stevenson. Inside, you'll be greeted by a spiral stone staircase that leads to a series of wood-paneled rooms, each packed with personal items owned by the trio of literary titans. Highlights include Burns's writing desk, a first edition of Scott's historical novel *Waverley*, and a wardrobe once owned by Stevenson; the latter was made by Deacon Brodie, a two-faced, thieving cabinetmaker believed to have been the inspiration for *The Strange Case of Dr. Jekyll and Mr. Hyde*. Makars' Court, just outside, is a lamplit courtyard, with flagstones etched with quotes by "makars" (writers and poets).

Lady Stair's Close, Old Town; cultureedinburgh.com

Scott Monument

It's impossible to miss the Scott Monument, a veritable Edinburgh icon. Standing at 200 ft (60 m) tall, this towering tribute to Sir Walter Scott is one of the world's largest monuments to a writer and was built following his death in 1832. Edinburgh locals, who funded the project, set up a competition to decide its design, and it was self-taught architect George Meikle Kemp who was the unlikely winner. His elegant Gothic masterpiece is sprinkled with statues depicting characters from Scott's novels, while at the base of the monument is a larger-than-life statue of the city's beloved writer, accompanied by Scott's loyal dog Maida. There's a little museum inside the monument, which has displays on Scott's life and literary works, and a 287-step staircase leading to a viewing platform that offers great views.

Princes Street Gardens East, Old Town; ewh.org.uk/the-scott-monument

Typewronger Books

Size, as they say, isn't everything, and Typewronger Books can prove it. This community-owned basement spot might be Edinburgh's smallest bookstore, but it still packs a punch, with a rotating list of more than 2,000 titles and an impressive range of genres (art, politics, poetry—you name it, they've probably got it). Spend some time browsing the collection, which includes indie publications and local zines, occasionally getting distracted by the gorgeous, old-school typewriters perched on the shelves and tables. This local hub also runs a host of events: think collaborative writing workshops, evening poetry readings and open-mic nights. But if simply browsing books is more your thing, you'll be pleased to hear there's more next door at McNaughtan's, Scotland's second-oldest antiquarian bookstore.

4a Haddington Place, New Town; typewronger.com

Topping & Company Booksellers

It's easy to lose hours in this homey bookstore, which covers two floors of a former 19th-century bank. For one thing, there are around 70,000 titles to discover. Genres run the gamut from Scottish history to sci-fi, with art, gardening, fantasy, and more nestled in between. The shop is a maze of floor-to-ceiling bookshelves, making it easy to lose yourself among the tomes. Nice touches include the *Beauty and the Beast*–style rolling library ladders (use them to reach the higher shelves), and the tables and chairs dotted here and there, where you can perch with a book and a free hot drink.

☞ 2 Blenheim Place, New Town; toppingbooks.co.uk

Armchair Books

Armchair Books promises a real sensory experience. There's that classic secondhand book smell as soon as you walk in; then, as you explore, you might just hear the quiet groan of bookshelves straining under the weight of so many titles, or the gentle murmur of passionate staff regaling tales of their favorite tomes to would-be buyers. The carpet is more than a little threadbare and much of the furniture has seen better days, but local bibliophiles couldn't care less. They're happy simply browsing the age-old books and walking through all that history.

☞ 72–74 West Port, Old Town; armchairbooks.co.uk

Topping & Company Booksellers

The Elephant House

The Elephant House

Often called the "Birthplace of Harry Potter," this crimson-fronted café on George IV Bridge is a pilgrimage site for Potterheads. This was, after all, a regular hangout spot for J. K. Rowling when she was penning the first two books about the now-famous boy wizard. But the café wasn't just a place to write—it also ignited her imagination, with the views of Edinburgh Castle, seen from her favorite window seat, inspiring the creation of Hogwarts School of Witchcraft and Wizardry. Other nearby sights also made their mark: charming Victoria Street, lined with colorful shop fronts, helped bring Diagon Alley to life, while the weathered gravestones in Greyfriars Kirkyard provided names for Tom Riddle (aka Lord Voldemort) and Professor McGonagall. With all that in mind, Edinburgh is the perfect place for a Potter pilgrimage.

☞ 30 Victoria Street, Old Town; elephanthouse.biz

Tills Bookshop

Perched on a corner overlooking the leafy Meadows park, teal-blue Tills was opened in 1986 and today is one of Edinburgh's oldest secondhand bookstores. There's no need to dig through big boxes or tottering piles of books here, though—everything in this charming, tiny shop is in its place. Shelves display a diverse range of well-organized books, including literary fiction and classic children's tales, plus poetry, philosophy, and a great collection of rare and antiquarian titles. Get comfy with a book on the window seat in the back room, which is warmed by a roaring fire during the winter months, or chat with one of the friendly staff, who are eager to help—and will likely encourage you to come along to the shop's laid-back Sunday book club.

☞ 1 Hope Park Crescent, Marchmont; tillsbookshop.co.uk

AUTHOR PROFILE

Muriel Spark

Famed for her sparse prose and compelling characters, Muriel Spark was born (1918) and raised in Edinburgh. Her first novel, the witty, wacky *The Comforters*, was published in 1957. Over the next five decades she published 21 novels, employing her characteristically economical prose and satirical tone. She died in Tuscany, Italy, in 2006.

Tills Bookshop

The Old Library, Trinity College

Dublin

IRELAND | EUROPE

Dublin is a writers' city. Whether you're walking in the footsteps of characters from classic Irish novels or mingling with those scribbling in notebooks in bookstore cafés, you'll feel the literary spirit steeped in the Irish capital's very bones.

It's hard to avoid the literary scene when you're in Dublin (not that you'd want to, of course). Known for its penchant for fun—better known here as *craic*—the Irish capital also has some serious literary credentials: this is a city that's produced some of the world's greatest writers, from James Joyce and Oscar Wilde to Anne Enright and Sally Rooney. And if you walk through almost any part of town (past Georgian-era houses, leafy parks, and riverside paths), you'll see blue plaques on the red-brick walls, marking the spots where writers like these once lived. They've left their mark all over the city, from the libraries where they once studied to the private "snug" in Toners, a pub that poet W. B. Yeats would frequent.

The old literary masters might hog the limelight, but there's also space for Dublin's up-and-coming writers, whether they're launching their work in a tiny bookstore or taking part in one of the city's numerous literary festivals. In recent years, there's also been a resurgence in the Gaelic tradition of the *seanchaí* (storyteller), with events held for writers—or anyone with a story in them—to stand up and share. And if you're at your happiest in an overstuffed bookstore, you're in luck—there are plenty scattered around the Liffey River.

GETTING AROUND

Dublin's center is very walkable, so unless you're venturing farther afield (say, to the James Joyce Tower in Sandycove), you won't need public transit. If you do, hop on a coastal Dart train or a Luas (tram).

READING LIST

Normal People

Sally Rooney

Read between the lines of the love story between Marianne and Connell and you'll uncover the subtleties of class and the complexities of family and friendship.

Montpelier Parade

Karl Geary

Geary's debut is a haunting story of an affair between a teenage boy and an older woman; it's set in Dublin during the 1980s.

Ulysses

James Joyce

Everyone knows it, but has everyone read it? Unlikely. Famed as one of the hardest English-language novels to read, Joyce's sprawling epic takes place over a single day in Dublin. Many of the sights mentioned in the book can still be visited today.

The Old Library, Trinity College

There's always a hushed sense of awe (and more than a few jostling elbows) when you stand before the *Book of Kells*. More than 1,225 years old, this ancient manuscript is one of the most famous books in the world, created by monks on the Scottish island of Iona and filled with delicate, intricate illustrations. But as impressive as it is, the atmospheric Long Room in the Old Library—where the book is displayed—is the cherry on top. With a giant, barrel-vaulted ceiling and two symmetrical lines of dark-wood bookshelves on either side, this is the library of every bookworm's fantasies. The fact that it's at Trinity College (the Irish capital's celebrated university) makes it all the sweeter—this is where authors Oscar Wilde, Bram Stoker, and Samuel Beckett all studied. Fans of Sally Rooney will also recognize the quad and historic grounds from the BBC adaptation of *Normal People*.

Trinity College, College Green, City Centre; visittrinity.ie

Museum of Literature Ireland

It's only fitting that Dublin's literary museum is set in the college building where James Joyce studied. But this is far from an ode to just one figure; instead, the Museum of Literature Ireland celebrates a host of Irish writers, from the classic to the contemporary. You might see 20th-century poet Brendan Behan's typewriter in the old Georgian part of the building, or the words from modern romance novels projected onto the walls in the gallery—all work is equal here. On the first Friday of the month, the museum opens late and entry is free, with live music, readings and themed events. Unsurprisingly, the gift shop is also top notch, as are the peaceful gardens at the back, where you can read under the same tree where Joyce had his graduation photo taken.

86 St. Stephen's Green, City Centre; moli.ie

Oscar Wilde House and Statue

There aren't many doorways as cluttered with memorial plaques as this one. That's because this townhouse, where Oscar Wilde was raised, doesn't only celebrate the Irish icon. Wilde's parents are also recognized: his mother was a renegade nationalist poet, while his father was a renowned surgeon. The building is now the campus for the American College Dublin (whose students have the luck of studying in such hallowed halls). However, on weekends and during academic holidays, visitors can take a tour of the house, accompanied by a knowledgeable guide with many a raucous tale of Wilde's youth to tell. Just across the road, on the corner of Merrion Square, is a flamboyant statue of the man, carved from precious stones and surrounded by plinths inscribed with Wilde quotes selected by the likes of Bono and Seamus Heaney.

1 Merrion Square, City Centre; oscarwildehouse.com

Books Upstairs

From the main entrance, this local favorite seems like a typical, everyday bookstore, with shelves stocked neatly with glossy new paperbacks and bestsellers. Move to the second level, however, and Books Upstairs' eccentric side breaks free. True to the name, there are, in fact, books upstairs, and they're far from orderly. The staircase is littered with stacks of secondhand novels, and side rooms overflow with titles it would take you a week to sift through. There are battered armchairs next to piles of books that resemble the Leaning Tower of Pisa, and mystery novels wrapped in newspaper, with cryptic notes hinting at their premises. And then there's the café, a Wi-Fi-free zone beloved by Dublin's avid readers. Join them by the stained-glass windows, poring over their new purchases and catching up over artisan toasted sandwiches.

17 D'Olier Street, City Centre; booksupstairs.ie

Ulysses Rare Books

If you're on the lookout for a first edition of *A Clockwork Orange* or a signed copy of *The Witches*, Ulysses Rare Books is the place to get it. This tiny shop isn't the kind that you can lose hours in, but it does have a strong collection of Irish greats, like poetry from Samuel Beckett and eye-wateringly expensive books signed by Oscar Wilde. But there are also more accessibly priced novels here—the perfect gift, perhaps, for the fellow book lover in your life. After you've explored the shelves, head next door for more literary history. Here you'll find The Duke, a classic Dublin watering hole that was frequented by Irish writers Patrick Kavanagh, Brendan Behan, and George Bernard Shaw, back in the day.

☞ 10 Duke Street, City Centre; rarebooks.ie

Ulysses Rare Books

Marsh's Library

Barely a thing has changed inside Marsh's Library since it opened in 1707. The same ladders lean against the shelves that groan under the weight of thick, leather-bound books. The floors still creak underfoot, and the ornate, cell-like reading cages—added in 1708 to prevent book theft—still remain, though people like Bram Stoker are no longer locked in there to do their reading. Speaking of Stoker, thanks to the library's thorough documentation, fans can find a list of all the books he read here as a teenager on the library's website (spot the maps of Transylvania). Smaller and quieter than the Long Room in Trinity, Marsh's Library is every bit as intoxicating. Be sure to chat with the on-site librarians, who can show you the books peppered with bullet holes from machine gun fire during the Easter Rising, or tell you their own experiences with the resident ghost.

☞ St. Patrick's Close, Liberties; marshlibrary.ie

AUTHOR PROFILE

James Joyce

Few writers are as closely associated with the Irish capital as James Joyce (1882–1941). Many of the Dublin-born writer's books (known for their use of stream of consciousness and wordplay) are set in the city. There's even a festival, Bloomsday, held every year to celebrate *Ulysses*. Joyce actually spent much of his life out of Ireland—in Trieste, Paris, London, and later in Zurich, where he died.

Shakespeare and Company

Paris

FRANCE | EUROPE

The City of Light has long been a beacon for literary luminaries. Like moths to a flame, creatives have flocked to the endlessly inspiring French capital; they've strolled its scenic streets, waxed lyrical in its cafés, and shaped the city for generations to come.

Somewhere as splendid as Paris needs little introduction. Since time immemorial, the City of Light (and Love) has been a place where writers, artists, and poets have come to muse. Why? Because it's impossible not to romanticize life here. Books like Victor Hugo's Gothic masterpiece *The Hunchback of Notre-Dame* have mythologized Paris's landmarks, but the small things hold as much sway. Daily banalities seem stylized in the French capital, from the musical lilt of police sirens to the buttery smell of fresh croissants at dawn. A playground for dreamers and storytellers alike, even the street-facing seats on café patios encourage you to notice the little details. And that's nothing new. Both French and expat authors—especially Americans from the Lost Generation, including F. Scott Fitzgerald and Ernest Hemingway, in the 1920s—have frequented Paris's coffee houses, mapping out big ideas over a few Gitanes.

Then there's the backbone of centuries of French literary culture propping up the city, immortalized by libraries so decadent you might think you need to be royalty to get in (you don't). Combine this with several world-renowned bookshops that still attract budding writers, and that's why Paris is, and always will be, a place you can't help but fall in love with.

GETTING AROUND

Central Paris is famously compact and (mostly) flat, meaning it's a dream to potter about on foot or bike. For slightly longer journeys, the city's 16 metro lines are quick and user-friendly.

READING LIST

Down and Out in Paris and London

George Orwell

This autobiographical account of Orwell's time in Paris and London portrays the poverty rampant in both cities during the 1930s.

Giovanni's Room

James Baldwin

The tragic tale of an American man living in Paris and his relationships with other men, Baldwin's masterpiece delves into the complexities of homosexuality, masculinity, and isolation.

The Hunchback of Notre-Dame

Victor Hugo

Hugo's love letter to the city's grand cathedral, this Gothic classic also interrogates themes of love, prejudice, and ableism in 15th-century Paris.

Shakespeare and Company

Shakespeare and Company

Often ranked as the world's most famous bookstore—with an equally iconic tote bag—this bohemian haunt is on every book lover's bucket list. Once you've made it past the famed green-and-gold frontage, everything points you toward the past, from the flaky plasterboard to the wooden eaves levitating over thousands of books. It all began when American bookseller George Whitman set up shop in 1951, renaming it in 1964 as a tribute to Sylvia Beach's legendary shop that once stood around the corner. Like its predecessor, Whitman's incarnation quickly attracted all manner of literary lights, including several Beat Generation authors like Allen Ginsberg and William S. Burroughs. Today, Sylvia Whitman maintains her father's open-door policy, inviting aspiring writers to sleep over in exchange for helping around the shop—you just wonder why they'd ever want to leave.

37 Rue de la Bûcherie, Latin Quarter; shakespeareandcompany.com

Bibliothèque Mazarine

France's oldest public library sits inside the Institut de France, which looks out across the Seine toward the Louvre. There's been a library here since 1643, when Cardinal Mazarin sought a place for his own private collections. Today, it houses around 600,000 rare items and promises a particularly gorgeous reading room. Gilded copper chandeliers hang from the ceiling of this rectangular space, while antique bronze busts look out with a hushed gaze that says, "we've been here a while." It's opulent, regal, and (happily) free to visit.

23 Quai de Conti, 6th arrondissement; bibliotheque-mazarine.fr

AUTHOR PROFILE

Ernest Hemingway

The larger-than-life writer called Paris home between 1921 and 1928, joining his fellow American authors (known as the Lost Generation) seeking inspiration on the continent. His memoirs during that period were published posthumously as *A Moveable Feast* (1964), a bacchanalian but earnest account of expat life as a struggling journalist in the French capital during the 1920s.

The Abbey Bookshop

When Canadian bookseller Brian Spence founded this anglophone bookstore in 1989, he cast a spell over English literature lovers, from Paris and beyond. Fans came in throngs then, drawn by the magic of this tiny book nook, and they still come in now. Walking through its pretty doorway is like entering the wardrobe to Narnia. Instead of a snowy wonderland, the destination is a world where every conceivable space is crammed with English books. A tight staircase leads to a cellar—it's very sensory down here, a secret grotto where the smell of old books mingles with the slight chill of being underground. And in a lovely twist of serendipity, the shop resides on an ancient road where Paris's scribes used to ply their trade in the Middle Ages.

29 Rue de la Parcheminerie, Latin Quarter; abbeybookshop.org

The Abbey Bookshop

Bouquinistes

Few bookish spots are as iconic as the 900 little green stalls lining this 2-mile (3-km) stretch on either side of the Seine. Slinking along the riverbank under the gaze of Notre-Dame, around 240 *bouquinistes* (the name given to these secondhand book dealers) flog rarities including antique books, old postcards, and vintage journals. This practice goes way back—there's evidence of vendors peddling their wares on the city's bridges as long ago as the 16th century, with some stalls staying in the same family for generations. However, it wasn't until the mid-1800s that the *bouquinistes* found a permanent home here. Their ongoing contribution to Parisian cultural life was recognized in 1991, when the riverside patch was designated a UNESCO World Heritage site. Arguably, no literary trip to Paris is complete without a walk here.

Right Bank: between Pont Neuf and Pont Marie; Left Bank: between Pont Royal and Pont de la Tournelle

Librairie Galignani

Founded in 1801 by Giovanni Antonio Galignani—a man whose family name has a long lineage in bookselling—this elegant emporium provides the perfect juxtaposition to the Left Bank's eccentric vibes. (It also lays claim to being the first bookstore on the continent to sell English titles.) Sheltered by the arched colonnades on one of Paris's fanciest shopping streets, Librairie Galignani is, unsurprisingly, very bougie inside. Beautifully built bookshelves gracefully curve toward the enormous skylight, blending with the well-trampled parquet flooring underfoot, while large houseplants offer a leafy flourish at every turn. Yes, you get the odd tourist drifting in here, but most of the clientele are well-dressed locals. This is Paris chic writ large.

224 Rue de Rivoli, 1st arrondissement; galignani.fr

Salle Ovale, Bibliothèque nationale de France

Bibliothèque nationale de France

If this branch of France's national library is the crown of the country's literary scene, Salle Ovale (the main reading room) is the glistening jewel. Designed by architect Jean-Louis Pascal in 1897, this gigantic space is a true temple to books. Entering the reading room makes your head spin, its elliptical shape wrapped by enormous three-tiered bookshelves, each divided by sturdy Ionic columns. Above, natural light streams in through a glass ceiling gilded in gold leaf. Sixteen round openings (or oculi) encircle the vast skylight, peering down and creating an almost celestial quality. It's impressive and utterly dizzying. Curiously, of the 20,000 books here, 9,000 are a collection of comics from around the world. So, dig out a rare edition of *Asterix* and take a seat alongside eternal students and day-trippers out for a leisurely read.

5 Rue Vivienne, 2nd arrondissement; bnf.fr

BOOK AT BEDTIME

L'Hôtel

Formerly known as Hôtel d'Alsace, this boutiquey gem *(l-hotel.com)* was the last place Oscar Wilde called home. Rooms are lavish (think sultry mauves and floral wallpaper) and it's on the Left Bank, so several of Paris's bookish haunts are nearby.

Les Deux Magots

Let's be honest, you might have come to Paris for the books, but it'd be rude not to try the food. One place that combines both is Les Deux Magots, a century-or-so-old brasserie that earned its reputation as a popular hangout for the city's literary elite. The Art Deco furnishings are as chic as ever, and smartly dressed waiters still flit between tables with purpose. Picture perfect, really. It's quite surreal imagining James Joyce nursing a *café au lait* on one of the red-leather benches, or Albert Camus tucking into a sugary *tarte tatin* here. If you're still hungry, pop over the road to Café de Flore for a *digestif*; this grand old coffee house is where James Baldwin penned much of his semiautobiographical *Go Tell It on the Mountain* (1953).

6 Place Saint-Germain des Prés, 6th arrondissement; lesdeuxmagots.fr

Les Deux Magots

Maison de Victor Hugo

Maison de Victor Hugo

Paris's 4th arrondissement is often regarded as the capital's cultural hub. Fitting, then, that it's where you'll find the former home of a titan of French literature, Victor Hugo. In 1832, at the age of 30, the author moved into this apartment, living and writing here for 16 years before heading to Guernsey in self-imposed exile. Filled with homemade furniture, the well-preserved space gives you an intimate snapshot of the great author's life. A museum downstairs also displays an extensive collection of Hugo's drawings and manuscripts.

6 Place des Vosges, Marais; maisonsvictorhugo.paris.fr

La Closerie des Lilas

Gastronomic and literary worlds collide at this famous Montparnasse restaurant. Opened in 1847 as a simple brasserie, it gained notoriety as a spot where Ernest Hemingway would come to write short stories while working for the *Toronto Star* (keep your eyes peeled for the tiny plaque marking his favorite seat). However, countless other big names put pen to paper here too, including writers Émile Zola, Samuel Beckett, F. Scott Fitzgerald, and Ezra Pound. Years later, the space still exudes the Art Deco glam of the interwar years: immaculate button-tufted benches and a lavish conservatory welcome you to savor some (slightly pricey) Francophone dishes. And to this day, the restaurant upholds its heritage, awarding the annual Prix de la Closerie des Lilas to women authors writing in French. *Chef's kiss*

171 Boulevard du Montparnasse, 6th arrondissement; closeriedeslilas.fr

Librairie Jousseaume

Picture a Parisian bookstore and you might imagine something like Librairie Jousseaume. This historic secondhand bookstore features a gorgeous arched entryway, a stunning spiral staircase, and bookshelves lined with age-old tomes. It's been family-run for generations, first opening back in 1826 and specializing in secondhand books ever since. It's lovely inside, and equally so when you step outside: Librairie Jousseaume is located within Galerie Vivienne, a glorious Neo-Classical covered passageway. It's a treat for photographers, with its glassy ceilings, light-filled halls, and mosaic floors. Be sure to walk around once you've stopped by the bookstore—there are plenty more cute boutiques and cafés here.

45-46-47 Galerie Vivienne, 2nd arrondissement; librairiejousseaume.fr

WALKING TOUR

Père Lachaise Cemetery

Blanketing the 20th arrondissement, Paris's largest municipal cemetery is the final resting place of many famous figures, including a number of literary luminaries. A stroll along its tree-lined paths winds past countless tombstones, some decorated with offerings.

i

DISTANCE
1 mile (1.5 km)

WALKING TIME
Allow half an hour

NEAREST TRANSIT
Philippe Auguste station (on metro line 2) or Père Lachaise station (on metro lines 2 and 3)

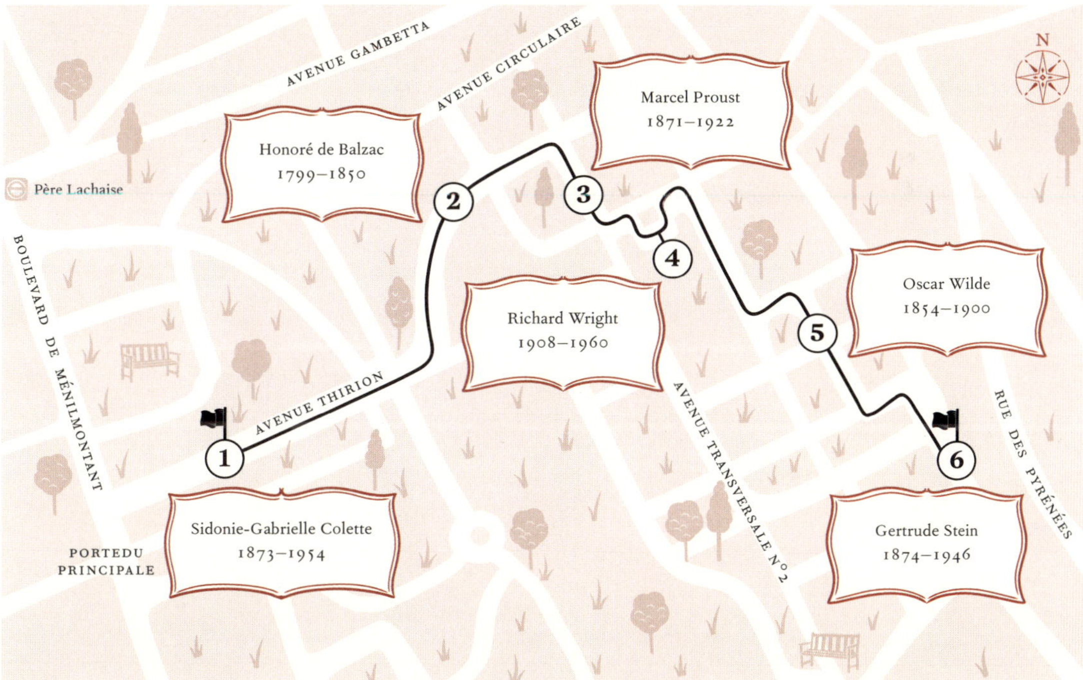

1. Sidonie-Gabrielle Colette

Novella author Sidonie-Gabrielle Colette—best known by her last name—was the first female writer in France to be given a state funeral. Her grave is often bedecked with flowers.

2. Honoré de Balzac

French novelist Honoré de Balzac loved to amble through Père Lachaise, so it seems fitting he was laid to rest here. A bronze bust of the writer marks his grave.

3. Marcel Proust

A black marble rectangle denotes the resting place of French author Marcel Proust. The grave is often topped with shell-shaped madeleine cakes, a nod to a scene from his novel *Swann's Way*.

4. Richard Wright

The ashes of African American novelist Richard Wright *(p.27)* are interred in the cemetery's Columbarium. The location is marked with a simple black stone inscribed with Wright's name.

5. Oscar Wilde

Wilde's *(p.108)* ornate tomb features a winged sphinx, once covered in lipstick kisses from his dedicated fans. Today, they leave kisses and notes on a glass screen instead.

6. Gertrude Stein

The Jewish American novelist and poet is buried with her partner, Alice B. Toklas. The pair lie beneath a granite gravestone, often topped with offerings of stones (a Jewish custom).

Cuesta de Moyano

Madrid

SPAIN | EUROPE

The Western novel was born in the Spanish capital, so it's unsurprising that Madrid is the country's most famous literary location. From Renaissance writings to Modernist movements, this dazzling city has played host to it all.

Welcome to the center of Spain. Elegant, culture-loving Madrid has celebrated good writing for centuries; well, since the 16th century at least, when the Castilian crown moved its courts to this erstwhile sleepy town and writers came flocking to entertain the growing population. A boom in poetry and theater followed, leading to heated battles of wits (16th-century rap battles) out on the streets from the likes of Spanish writers Lope de Vega, Calderón de la Barca, and Miguel de Cervantes. It was a Golden Age for both the city and the Castilian tongue, one crowned by the birth of the Western novel as we know it: *Don Quixote*, first published in 1605.

Later, in the 20th century, writers as disparate as Ernest Hemingway and Federico García Lorca found themselves and their voices in the hubbub of the city's café culture, chaotic streets, and social upheavals, which made Madrid one of Europe's most fervent literary stages. Acclaimed local writer Almudena Grandes *(p.122)* arguably ruled the early 21st century, but following her passing, space remains for a new master of Madrid's literary scene. Join local book lovers browsing quirky book markets and socializing at author events, and you might just meet them.

GETTING AROUND

While most of Madrid's literary sites are within easy walking distance of each other, the metro and bus network provide a convenient and affordable way to get around the city.

READING LIST

Don Quixote

Miguel de Cervantes

One of the world's most translated novels, this 17th-century tale follows a knight errant and his witty squire. You'll spot numerous monuments to the story and Cervantes while in Madrid.

The Hive

Camilo José Cela

Set over three days in 1943, this classic postwar novel depicts the struggles of a wide cast of characters living in Madrid during the first years of the dictatorship.

Bad Habit

Alana S. Portero

This gritty but tender coming-of-age tale follows the life of a young trans woman living in one of Madrid's neighborhoods during the heroin crisis of the 1980s and 1990s.

Cuesta de Moyano

Running down from the leafy Retiro Park beside the Royal Botanical Gardens—two perfect reading spots in their own right—Cuesta de Moyano is a pedestrian street lined with wooden stalls, all packed with books (primarily secondhand). A steady stroll while perusing their wares will put you in the company of great writers (the likes of Hemingway) and avid readers (such as the queen of Spain), who have been flocking here for more than a century now. Some stalls sell dusty tomes from specific centuries, some specialize in art—they are only a stone's throw from art icon Museo Nacional del Prado, after all—but what they all promise are great reading recommendations from booksellers who set up shop come rain or shine.

☞ Cuesta de Moyano, Jerónimos; soydelacuesta.org

Barrio de las Letras

Librería Desnivel

When you have to pull on an ice ax to get into a bookstore, you know you're in for something special. Librería Desnivel is a haven for ramblers, climbers, and outdoor enthusiasts, who head here to pick up guidebooks, maps, technical manuals, and travel literature, or to be inspired by talks from some of the most renowned mountaineers in the world. The climbing material and charming alpine decor are not exactly original features (the trekking twist is a more recent addition), but the shop holds the honor of being the longest-running bookstore in town. Another fun fact: the back half of the premises is actually a former paper warehouse and used to supply all the local printing presses in the city center.

☞ Plaza de Matute, 6, Barrio de las Letras; libreriadesnivel.com

Barrio de las Letras

Madrid's so-called "literary neighborhood" is self-explanatory. The colorful streets here are embossed with brass-cast quotes from famous Spanish writers who have called this quarter home over the last five centuries; the squares are decked with statues of local legends like Cervantes and Lorca; and you can even travel back to Spain's literary Golden Age by paying a visit to playwright Lope de Vega's former residence *(casamuseolopedevega.org)*. Cervantes also lived in the area (Calle de Cervantes, 2) until his death, but his house was sadly demolished. Despite being a mere stone's throw from the heart of the city (and many of its top museums), the tiled taverns, low-key tapas bars, and bijou boutiques here offer the quietude that any writer needs to get their quill flowing.

☞ Barrio de las Letras; esmadrid.com/barrios-de-madrid/barrio-letras

Biblioteca Nacional de España

Librería Miguel Miranda

Founded by a close friend of Basque literary giant Pío Baroja and a favorite haunt of Madrileño Nobel laureate Camilo José Cela, this antique bookstore has been passed down through the generations since the late 1940s. The family of *libreros*, starting with the eponymous Miguel Miranda, cut their teeth filling the "Spanish Lit" shelves of the Oxbridge and Ivy League libraries and important national collections, and to this day, the founder's grandson still provides a haven for lovers of ancient tomes and rare finds.

Calle de Lope de Vega, 19, Barrio de las Letras; libreriamiranda.com

Biblioteca Nacional de España

Dating back to 1711, the largest library in the Spanish-speaking world found its current home in this Neo-Classical masterpiece in the late 19th century. Today, its shelves hold tens of millions of items, including a giant *Don Quixote* collection (if you're hankering to lay your eyes on a first edition from 1605, you'll have to head to the library at the Palacio de Liria). With collections as grand as these, the library is naturally quite protective of its possessions, so visiting bookworms will need to sign up for a reader's card in advance to access most of the reading rooms.

Paseo de Recoletos, 20-22, Recoletos; bne.es

Librería San Ginés

Squirreled away down an alley and built onto the side of a church, Librería San Ginés—which looks more like an ancient fruit stand than a bookstore—has been selling tomes since way back in 1650. Bookish history spills out beyond its ramshackle walls too, as the alley curves round to Chocolatería San Ginés, not only Madrid's favorite churros spot but also one of the settings for Ramón de Valle-Inclán's play *Lights of Bohemia* and parts of Benito Pérez Galdós's novel cycle, *National Episodes*. Despite their lauded history, both institutions are slowly giving in to the modern world: the café buzzes with tourists, and the book stand sells souvenirs, but there's still plenty of old-world charm to be found.

Pasadizo de San Ginés, 2, Sol

AUTHOR PROFILE

Almudena Grandes

Despite remaining relatively unknown and under-translated in the English-speaking world, Almudena Grandes is one of the Spanish capital's most beloved authors—so much so that Madrid's main train station was named after her following her passing in 2021. Her epics on the upheavals of recent Spanish history captivated audiences—expect harrowing realism and intimate psychological portraits.

Librería San Ginés

La Pecera del Círculo de Bellas Artes

If La Pecera's fresco ceilings, grand columns, and chandeliers could talk, oh, the stories they'd tell of feisty debates among the likes of Pablo Picasso, Nobel-winner Jacinto Benavente, and anarchist playwright Valle-Inclán (the latter once called for the whole building to be burned down). While Paris's literary salons found their place in private residences, Madrid's equivalent, its *tertulias*, took place in bars and cafés, and La Pecera is one of those spots. The name translates as "the goldfish bowl" or, less literally, the place where writers, artists, and intellectuals would gather to see and be seen. Located in the city's Art Deco complex for all things creative, El Círculo de Bellas Artes, this lavishly decorated café-restaurant was founded a century ago as a "conversation hall" by none other than the king of Spain himself (so the story goes), and the creative discussions haven't stopped since then.

Calle de Alcalá, 42, Cortes;
circulobellasartes.com/restauracion/la-pecera

Residencia de Estudiantes

Just as the Barrio de las Letras formed the crucible of the intellectual fervor of the Spanish literary Golden Age, the Residencia de Estudiantes—the former student halls of Madrid—nurtured the awakening of the country's Silver Age, that early-20th-century renaissance of artistic innovation and scientific creativity. Iberian greats such as Federico García Lorca, Salvador Dalí, and Luis Buñuel called this place home back in their university days, but now their former dorms host both traveling intellectuals and a range of literary events. Time your visit for a talk or exhibition, or simply drop by to peek at a re-creation of an old student dorm and dine in the same spot where folks like Marie Curie once ate.

Calle del Pinar, 21-23, Chamartín;
residenciadeestudiantes.com

Cervantes Birthplace Museum

Cervantes Birthplace Museum

On the outskirts of Madrid lies the quiet university town of Alcalá de Henares, which, with its perfectly preserved colleges and abundance of bookstores, could easily be a bookish spot in its own right. Its highlight is the Cervantes Birthplace Museum, a modest, 16th-century house offering an intimate vision of the famed writer's world. For the complete Cervantes pilgrimage, visit during the town's annual Semana Cervantina: a celebration of the author that sits somewhere between a Renaissance fair and a literary festival.

Calle Mayor 48, Alcalá de Henares;
museocasanataldecervantes.org

A Brasileira

Lisbon

PORTUGAL | EUROPE

Walking through Lisbon feels like stepping into the pages of a well-worn novel. Blue-tiled buildings swoop over hills, narrow streets are lined with age-old cafés, and rickety wooden trams trundle along. In Portugal's capital, the story writes itself.

Lisbon is an easy place to fall in love with. Overlooking the sparkling waters of the Tagus River, this colorful hilltop capital promises scenic streets, thrilling viewpoints, world-famous foodie spots and (perhaps best of all) nearly 3,000 hours of sunshine a year. It's hard for the average visitor to resist the Portuguese capital's charms, but it's even harder for literary lovers. Amid the jumble of pretty streets lies a trove of grandiose libraries, street fairs selling worn tomes, trendy bookstores, and cafés steeped in bookish history.

Lisbon's literary roots go way back. It was here that Luís Vaz de Camões penned his epic poem *The Lusiads* in 1572, recounting the lives of Portugal's seafarers. Later came Eça de Queirós, who skewered the social mores of a decadent 19th-century Lisbon. Few, however, compare to the city's two modern greats: Fernando Pessoa—whose poems and prose meander through the city—and Lisboeta laureate José Saramago—who rewrote the capital's past and present as modern-day parables. Read any of their masterpieces and you'll feel like you're walking straight through the city. Better yet, visit yourself to wander the streets they walked; you'll soon realize why they too fell in love with Lisbon.

GETTING AROUND

While distances might seem short in Lisbon, those hills can be tough. Fortunately, iconic yellow trams, funicular railroads, and outdoor lifts are there to help with the inclines.

READING LIST

The Maias

Eça de Queirós

Often considered Portugal's great realist novel, this satirical portrait of Lisbon society exposes the decadence and moral drift of the late Portuguese monarchy.

The Book of Disquiet

Fernando Pessoa

Published decades after the author's death, this fragmentary anti-novel follows a solitary narrator as he wanders through Lisbon.

The History of the Siege of Lisbon

José Saramago

Set between modern Lisbon and its medieval past, Saramago's masterful work follows a proofreader who inserts a single word into a history book, reimagining the city's Reconquista and blurring the line between fact and fiction.

Livraria Bertrand

Livraria Bertrand

Let's be honest, there are probably quite a few bookstores around the world that claim to be the oldest, but only Livraria Bertrand has the Guinness World Record. This historic spot in Lisbon's lovely Chiado neighborhood has been going since 1732—which is no mean feat given that almost the entire city was destroyed a few years later by the 1755 earthquake. When you step in through the gorgeous, blue-tiled façade (a Lisbon classic), you'll see why Bertrand is still in business centuries later. Those grand wooden bookshelves, vaulted ceilings, and well-stocked shelves have kept customers coming back for centuries on end. Every room is named after a famous Portuguese writer, in case you need a little pointer on where to get started on your Lusophone lit.

☞ Rua Garrett 73–75, Chiado; bertrand.pt

A Brasileira

Marble surfaces, frescoed ceilings, waiters in waistcoats and ties: the glorious Art Nouveau A Brasileira café appears lost in another era. This beloved coffee shop even has its own *quiosque* (or newsstand) crafted in majestic hardwood, so do as the locals do and peruse a paper as you enjoy your strong *bica* (espresso) and *pastel de nata*. Of course, Lisboetas will tell you that the elegant Belém neighborhood is the place to go if you want to try the famous Portuguese pastry, but A Brasileira is definitely the most literary spot for one (or two). Don't believe us? Just ask iconic Portuguese poet, writer, and regular Fernando Pessoa—there's a bronze statue of him outside sipping on his Brasileira brew.

☞ Rua Garrett 120, Chiado; abrasileira.pt

Feira de Alfarrabistas

A stroll through the Feira da Ladra flea market, with all its glorious bric-a-brac, is practically a ritual for folks visiting Lisbon, but did you know there's also a literary equivalent? Chiado's Feira de Alfarrabistas takes place every Saturday morning, and it's a must for bookish travelers. In Portuguese *alfarrabista* translates to "antique book dealer" and that's precisely what you'll find here. A whole street, Rua da Anchieta to be precise, packed with ancient tomes and secondhand books at more-than-reasonable prices (there are rows upon rows of €1 items). As well as books, sellers also offer a host of posters, prints, and postcards—perfect if you're looking for a unique souvenir for the trip. Not in town on a Saturday? Not to worry, there's another used book fair in Jardim Constantino on Wednesday instead.

☞ Rua Anchieta, Chiado

Casa dos Bicos

If you're not familiar with the work of Lisbon legend José Saramago, get the lowdown at Casa dos Bicos. This quirky, 16th-century building features a Renaissance façade covered in bizarre spikes (the "bicos" of the name); it's a fittingly surreal setting, if you know Saramago. Inside, you'll find exhibits chronicling the Portuguese Nobel laureate's life and work, including first editions, manuscripts, and personal effects. Back outside, don't miss the olive tree in the middle of the road; it was brought in from Saramago's hometown of Azinhaga as a final resting place for his ashes.

Rua dos Bacalhoeiros 10, Alfama; josesaramago.org

Ler Devagar

A trip out to the Alcântara neighborhood will take you to LX Factory, a former textile mill that's now a trendy, creative complex packed with restaurants, galleries, studios, and one of the world's most impressive bookstores, Ler Devagar. A former warehouse measuring 46 ft (14 m) in height, this bookish haven is stacked high with industrial-chic shelves spanning various floors. The name, *ler devagar*, literally means "read slowly," and this is definitely a place to enjoy at a relaxed pace. Look around the different levels and browse titles both new and used. There's even a café inside, so you really can take your time.

Rua Rodrigues Faria 103, Alcântara; lerdevagar.com

Ler Devagar

Florence's Duomo

Florence

ITALY | EUROPE

The Renaissance capital has backdropped countless coming-of-age novels and romantic memoirs, but swooning under the Tuscan sun is mostly a 20th-century invention. The dark root of Florentine literary tradition lies in plagues and power-seekers.

Florentine storytelling is the stuff of legend. It was here, in the city's narrow medieval streets, that Dante Alighieri—known as the "Father of the Italian Language"—used the Florentine vernacular in place of formal Latin in his *Divine Comedy*, giving it literary value and laying the groundwork for modern Italian. That Florentines are storytellers at heart was later implied in Giovanni Boccaccio's *Decameron*, which colorfully recounted a quarantine during the Black Death, made more bearable by friends telling tales. Literature continued to flourish during the Renaissance, when Florence became a creative capital under the patronage of the Medici family. And at the end of this prosperous period came Florentine diplomat Niccolò Machiavelli, whose *The Prince* exposed the deception at the heart of politics, showing the world how stories get spun, not just told.

Tough acts to follow, but in the centuries since, Florence has birthed more writers (Vasco Pratolini and Oriana Fallaci), and its painterly beauty has lured even more of them (Henry James and Elizabeth Barrett Browning). Today this legacy plays out all over the city, in corner bookstores and Chianti-fueled poetry readings, acclaimed literary prizes and story-forward festivals. Perhaps another Renaissance is looming.

GETTING AROUND

Italians sometimes call Florence *una città a misura d'uomo* (a human-sized city). Buses and trams are available and inexpensive, but walking is the most pleasant (and efficient) option.

READING LIST

The Decameron

Giovanni Boccaccio

A classic collection of tales covering love, adventure, life, and death, told through the voices of young Florentines quarantining during the Black Death.

A Room with a View

E. M. Forster

Florence is sweltering and swoon-worthy in E. M. Forster's romantic classic, which takes young Lucy on a transformative trip to the city. Set during the early 20th century, it offers a witty critique of a stuffy English society.

Still Life

Sarah Winman

An instant hit, *Still Life* follows an unlikely circle of friends tracing their lives and relationships as they unfold over decades between Florence and East London.

Casa Guidi

How did the Browning poets love Florence? Let us count the ways. In line with their romantic sensibilities, Robert and Elizabeth Barrett Browning lived in the Renaissance city from 1847 until 1861, settling in this unassuming home around the corner from the Pitti Palace. Though Elizabeth was bedridden for much of their time here, it was a productive period for the couple, in part due to their interest in the Risorgimento (Italian unification) cause. The movement inspired Elizabeth's novel-length poem "Casa Guidi Windows," drawn from the unrest brewing outside her bedroom window. The pair lived here until Elizabeth died; she was buried in the English Cemetery in Piazzale Donatello. Fans can drop by to talk to the cemetery's caretaker, Julia Bolton Holloway, a veritable expert on the Brownings.

☞ Piazza San Felice 8, Oltrarno; cultura.gov.it

Giunti Odeon

Giunti Odeon

"Chi vuol essere lieto, sia / Di doman' non c'è certezza." (Whoever wants to be happy, let them be: tomorrow is not guaranteed.) In gold lettering, this verse from Lorenzo de' Medici's "A Song for Bacchus" towers over the movie screen anchoring the Giunti Odeon—a grand cinema, bookstore, café, and event space housed in an old Art Nouveau theater. "Tomorrow" wasn't guaranteed for the struggling, century-old theater, until it entered a new era under Giunti, a born-in-Florence publishing house and bookstore chain. Since 2023, the venue has balanced its longtime film focus with bookish pursuits, hosting author presentations and other events. By day, students and remote workers curl up in the original gold velvet seats in the balcony. By night, the upper level of Giunti Odeon transforms back into a cinema, specializing in films shown in their original language with Italian subtitles (a rarity in Italy).

☞ Via degli Anselmi 3-5-7, Piazza Strozzi; giuntiodeon.com

Todo Modo

Perched on the gallery- and antiques-strewn Via de' Fossi, Todo Modo looks like little more than a hole in the wall. Step inside, however, and the space expands into a buzzy shop and café (complete with natural wines and international titles) and a large reading room (where students halfheartedly do homework and friends catch up under the guise of magazine reading). The room has also hosted talks from authors like Sally Rooney and Olga Tokarczuk. Owners Pietro and Maddalena are a charismatic couple with eclectic interests, and their spin-off projects include Todo Modo Dilà, a shop for young readers (Via dei Serragli 18r), and a Japanese book-lined bento bar, Hiroko Bentō e Vini Fatti a Modo (Piazza Morvillo 46).

☞ Via dei Fossi 15r, Santa Maria Novella; todomodo.org

The British Institute of Florence

The British Institute of Florence

Stretching back to the days of the Grand Tour—when young European aristocrats traveled around cultural capitals—the British have a history of cultural exchange with Italy, which may be more pronounced in Florence than anywhere else. Affectionately known as *il British*, this cultural institute is best known for the Harold Acton Library, named after the eponymous British aesthete and a hub for English-language lectures on Italian culture. Best of all, for those moments when espresso just won't do, there's a proper afternoon tea (usually the first Wednesday of the month) for a small donation.

Lungarno Guicciardini 9, Oltrarno; britishinstitute.it

Paperback Exchange

When it was time for Maurizio and Emily—the beloved couple who founded "PapEx" in the 1970s—to retire and sell Florence's premier English-language bookstore some 40 years later, devoted fans were more than a little anxious about its fate. Thankfully, the pair were adamant that their buyer preserve its bookish spirit. That's how it came into the care of duo Icaro and Gianluca, who are committed to the original mission, while also enlivening the space with signings and author talks. Inside, it's small but dense, and far superior to the English sections found in most big-box book retailers in Florence.

Via delle Oche 4r, Duomo; papex.it

Piccola Farmacia Letteraria

Grieving a loved one? On the cusp of a new relationship and feeling trepidatious? Certain states of mind or matters of the heart call for certain types of books. This idea of reading-as-remedy is the foundation of Elena Mulino's "Little Literary Pharmacy," which has charmed Florentines and visitors alike since its opening in 2018, offering "literary solutions for real problems." Books are shelved and color-coded according to emotions, and the shop is committed to its "pharmacy" theme: descriptions even veer into possible side effects of finishing this-or-that classic romance or page-turning hero's journey.

☞ Via del Castellaccio 45r, Duomo; piccolafarmacialetteraria.it

Biblioteca Marucelliana

Florence is filled with monuments made possible by great fortunes, but it was never a city for the wealthy few; in fact, democratization—of knowledge, art, and beauty—is at the core of the city's identity. The walnut-bookshelved Biblioteca Marucelliana, created at the behest of bibliographer and abbot Francesco Marucelli (1625–1703), is proof. Your first clue is in the façade's inscription: *Maxime Pauperum Utilitati*, or "especially for the use of the poor." In his last will and testament, Marucelli called for the foundation of a new library, bequeathing it his own collection, on the (revolutionary!) condition that everyone would have access. And they still do today.

☞ Via Cavour 43, Duomo/San Marco; marucelliana.cultura.gov.it

Biblioteca Marucelliana

WALKING TOUR

Dante's Florence

Florence's historic center looks quite different than it did in medieval times, when Dante walked the streets. Yet given the writer's lasting legacy, you'll find traces of his life all over the city—along the Arno River's edge, at key central monuments and buried down narrow backstreets.

DISTANCE
1 mile (1.5 km)

WALKING TIME
Allow half an hour

NEAREST TRANSIT
Buses (the 6, 36 and C3) connect this area of the city, though most people explore on foot

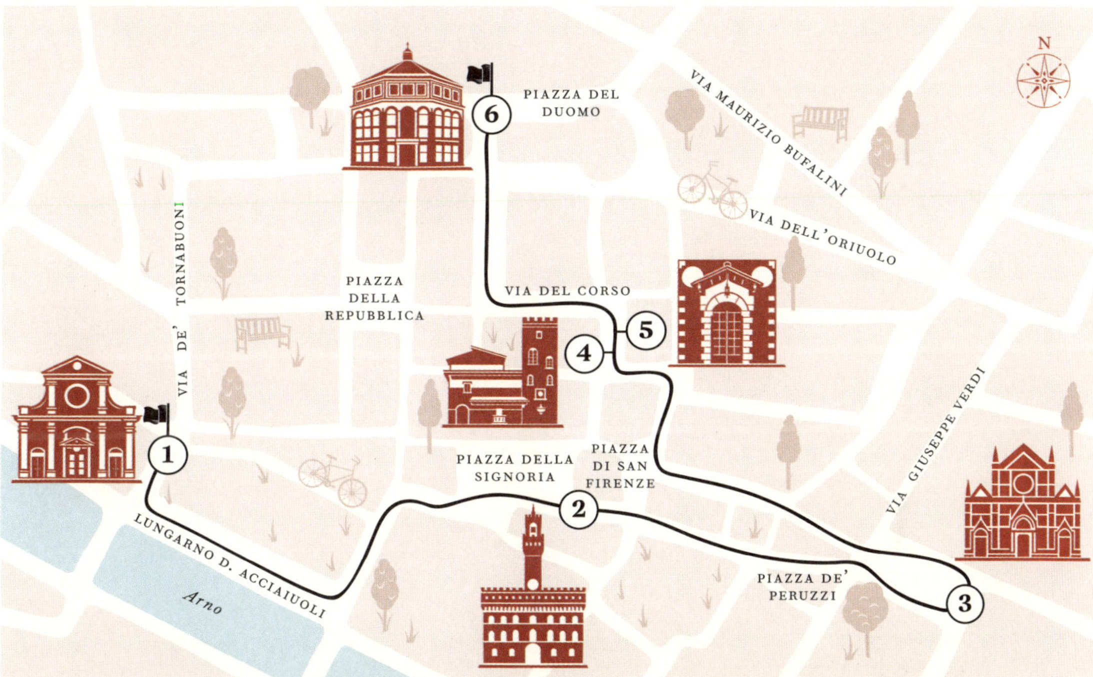

1. Basilica di Santa Trinita

Dante is said to have been sentenced to exile here. The charge was financial corruption, but it was likely a result of his opposition to papal interference in local politics *(Piazza di Santa Trinita)*.

2. Palazzo Vecchio

This is the seat of Florentine civic government and a working museum. The collection highlight? Dante's striking funerary mask, made famous by Dan Brown's novel *Inferno*.

3. Basilica di Santa Croce

Dante is buried in Ravenna, Italy, where he died in exile, but Florence won't quite accept that as his final resting place. An empty tomb awaits his homecoming in this church *(Piazza di Santa Croce, 16)*.

4. Casa di Dante

Dante was born in the area around this charming house-museum, which reproduces elements of the Alighieri family home and sheds light on his complicated life *(Via Santa Margherita, 1)*.

5. Santa Margherita dei Cerchi

This is widely regarded as the site where Dante first met his great love, Beatrice Portinari; a plaque names it "Dante's church" *(Via Santa Margherita, 4/6r)*.

6. Baptistery of Florence

This Florentine icon gets name-checked in the *Divine Comedy* as "my beautiful San Giovanni" (Canto 19, *Inferno*). Young Dante was baptized here in 1266 *(Piazza San Giovanni)*.

Österreichische Nationalbibliothek

Vienna

AUSTRIA | EUROPE

In this most grand of European cities, a strong literary legacy sits alongside a heritage of art, architecture, and music. Here, resplendent coffee houses and age-old libraries rub shoulders with contemporary bookstores.

Capital of the powerful Hapsburg Empire for almost 250 years, Vienna promises stunning Imperial architecture, musical legacy, and art-filled museums, plus an illustrious literary past. At the turn of the 20th century, against a backdrop of political and economic uncertainty, Vienna's coffee houses became hotbeds of discussion and debate. A whole host of famous thinkers passed through their doors, among them Communist writer Leon Trotsky, psychoanalyst Sigmund Freud, and author Franz Kafka. Others included the novelists Stefan Zweig and Robert Musil, whose works captured the unease of an age when the Austro-Hungarian Empire was in decline. Since then, other Viennese-based writers have taken up their pens, with Thomas Bernhard and Elfriede Jelinek (who won the Nobel Prize in Literature in 2004) exploring the city's dark undercurrents.

Today, Vienna's grand coffee houses continue to inspire a new generation of thinkers, as do the city's libraries, among them the magnificent Österreichische Nationalbibliothek, and its modern bookstores, which burst with new ideas. With such draws, it's no wonder that curious and cultured Vienna continues to be a hangout for the literary-minded.

GETTING AROUND

Vienna is a great place for a stroll, especially around its historic center. The city also has an excellent public transportation system, comprising bus, tram, and U-Bahn (subway).

READING LIST

The World of Yesterday

Stefan Zweig

This classic memoir paints a picture of Viennese society in the early 20th century, at the end of the Austro-Hungarian Empire.

The Piano Teacher

Elfriede Jelinek

A haunting masterpiece that follows Erika Kohut, who teaches piano at the Vienna Conservatory by day and trawls the porn shows of the city by night.

The Woodcutters

Thomas Bernhard

In a meandering rant about the vanity and moral emptiness of the cultural elite, this bitterly comic monologue follows a narrator enduring a Viennese funeral dinner party.

Österreichische Nationalbibliothek

Housed in the vast Hofburg Palace, the Austrian National Library is a Baroque masterpiece. At its center lies the State Hall, a soaring space supported by marble columns and crowned with a frescoed dome. This cathedral to literature is home to around 200,000 leather-bound tomes (although there are over 12 million items in the library's collection), which are neatly tucked into the gleaming wooden bookshelves, set across two levels (the upper level is inaccessible to visitors). Don't miss the library's Literature Museum, a short walk away, which traces the country's literary past from the Enlightenment to modern times, placing key authors and their works in historical context. Most of the information is in German, so grab a tablet from the ticket counter to allow you to access English translations.

☞ Josefsplatz 1, Innere Stadt; onb.ac.at

Österreichische Nationalbibliothek

ChickLit

It's true that Vienna, with its wide boulevards lined by imposing Baroque buildings, can often feel overly formal, even aloof. The antidote? A trip to ChickLit. Popping into this queer-feminist bookstore feels like wandering into a friend's cozy living room: expect scuffed wooden floors, comfy chairs and mismatched lamps; there's a friendly dog to welcome you in, too. The shop (which has its finger firmly on the pulse of the contemporary literary scene) specializes in queer and feminist texts, as well as books by women writers, with many options in English. It also has a great range of zines and graphic novels—a good way to brush up your German (a picture speaks a thousand words and all that). The friendly, knowledgeable staff are more than happy to give recommendations, so expect to leave here with a bulging bag of books.

☞ Kleeblattgasse 7, Innere Stadt; chicklit.at

Freud Museum

Sigmund Freud wrote over 20 books during his lifetime, with *The Interpretation of Dreams*—the text that established his theories of psychoanalysis—being the most famous. His former residence and offices, hidden behind an unassuming door at Berggasse 19, are now open to visitors—although to enter you'll have to put yourself in the shoes of famous case studies like Little Hans or the Wolf Man and ring the doorbell. As you step inside, the rooms of the museum might feel almost uncannily sparse; that's because Freud managed to escape Austria with most of his library and furniture in tow (yes, even *that* iconic chaise lounge). That's not a bad thing, though: it just means that there's plenty of space for the museum's enthralling displays on the life and works of the founding father of psychoanalysis.

☞ Berggasse 19, Alsergrund; freud-museum.at

Café Central

Where better to enjoy a slice of Vienna's fin-de-siècle romance than Café Central? Found in a former palatial bank building, this coffee house is one of the city's most famous, with a grand interior of vaulted ceilings, glowing chandeliers, and polished wooden floors. This opulent spot holds extra allure for book lovers, as the café was once a hangout for local literati such as Stefan Zweig, Karl Kraus, and Hugo von Hofmannsthal, who would come here to discuss ideas and to fuel their writing with coffee and a cake. Follow in their footsteps by ordering a *melange* (Vienna's answer to the cappuccino) and one of the beautifully made sweet treats, then sit back to soak in the atmosphere. If you can't get a table (with everyone wanting their slice of history and strudel, it can get pretty busy here), then head over to nearby Café Landtmann, a favorite haunt of German novelist Thomas Mann.

Herrengasse 14, Innere Stadt; cafecentral.wien

Café Central

Phil

Quirkily decorated, with posters and vinyl on the walls and a clash of lights hanging from the ceiling (there's even a disco ball), it's fair to say that eclectic vibes are the name of the game at this cool bookstore café. The collection of titles for sale is no different from the decor: arranged neatly on the wooden shelves, the books here include everything from contemporary novels to travel titles, biographies, art books, and kids' reads. The shop's literary ethos is summed up in a single quote attached to one of the shelves: "Don't classify me, read me. I'm a book, not a genre." Spend some time browsing for your next read, then grab a coffee or a kombucha and plonk yourself down on one of the gorgeous leather sofas to soak in the friendly, laid-back vibes.

Gumpendorfer Straße 10–12, Mariahilf; cafephil.at

BOOK AT BEDTIME

Altstadt Vienna

Each of the 62 rooms in this boutique hotel *(altstadt.at)* near the Museums-Quartier has a different theme, with the Library Suite being one for book lovers. Here, a curved iron staircase leads to a mini library; there's even a writing desk, if inspiration strikes.

Saint-Pierre-de-Clages

Saint-Pierre-de-Clages

SWITZERLAND | EUROPE

Nestled in the heart of the Swiss Alps, Saint-Pierre-de-Clages is famed for two things: its 12th-century stone church and a deep love of books. In fact, this tiny little town—whose population numbers around 800—is the only "book town" in Switzerland. Its collection of secondhand independent bookstores is popular year-round, while late summer sees its streets come alive for a jam-packed literary festival.

L'Escapade

Run by the passionate folks who set up the Fête du Livre, L'Escapade has a great range of secondhand titles, including some gorgeous rare and antique volumes.

Espace Arvoisie, Rue du Prieuré 21

Bouquinerie de La Potagère

This secondhand bookstore is part of La Potagère, a buzzing community hub that also contains a concert hall, vegetable shop, and bar-brasserie. All profits go to supporting children with cancer.

Rue de l'Eglise 3

Le Fouineur

A stone's throw from the town's church, Le Fouineur is packed with over 150,000 books ranging from cooking to philosophy to sports. Expect a few rare titles, too.

lefouineur.ch

La Musette

Books meet vinyl at tiny La Musette, which is crammed with both new and used offerings. The cozy space holds regular events, such as readings and poetry evenings.

34 Rue de l'Eglise

Watched over by soaring mountains and surrounded by vineyards, picturesque Saint-Pierre-de-Clages has existed since the Middle Ages, but it wasn't until the early 1990s that it gained fame as a literary destination. It was all thanks to a group of bookish locals, who—inspired by the likes of Hay-on-Wye *(p.92)* and the Belgium book village of Redu—decided their home would be a "book town." To kick things off, they set up a literary festival (with advice from Hay's own Richard Booth).

Come August, the three-day Fête du Livre draws some 20,000 book lovers to the town for book signings, author readings, and literary-inspired art, plus activities like bookbinding and calligraphy. The success of the festival has also lured more booksellers to the town, and today their welcoming secondhand bookstores dot the charming streets.

Fête du Livre

Jacob-und-Wilhelm-Grimm-Zentrum

Berlin

GERMANY | EUROPE

Progressive and proudly radical, modern Berlin is a place where experimentation is encouraged. Pair this with a past characterized by both freedom and tyranny, and it's no surprise that this complicated capital is a hotbed for literary expression.

It's impossible to overlook the extent to which Berlin's history is etched into literary culture. Unlike many other European capitals, where yesteryear feels distant and obscure, the embers of the past still smolder here. Berlin's Weimar years (1918–1933) created an environment ripe for artists, its raucous cabaret clubs and raw hedonism inspiring the likes of writers Christopher Isherwood and Alfred Döblin. The party ended abruptly in the 1930s, when the National Socialists snatched power. Local writer Hans Fallada and, more recently, Scottish author Philip Kerr captured the tense danger and censorship of those dark days. In the rubble of World War II, Berlin was divided both physically and ideologically, a bleak backdrop eternalized in many of John le Carré's spy novels.

Berlin is quite different today. The city in the 21st century is forward-thinking, inclusive, and intent on learning from its past. Hulking great libraries abound, architectural wonders in their own right and packed with students eager to consume knowledge. Meanwhile, quirky bookstores line the streets, each one unique. Some specialize in secondhand books, some feminist criticism, some simply pack the shelves with whatever they want; the message is the same regardless: knowledge is power.

GETTING AROUND

Berlin has an extensive and reliable public transportation network. Most neighborhoods are well connected by the U-Bahn (underground), S-Bahn (commuter train), bus, or tram.

READING LIST

Alone in Berlin

Hans Fallada

Fallada's bestseller is based on the true story of a working-class couple, Otto and Elise Hampel, who launched a silent campaign of defiance against the Nazi regime in wartime Berlin.

Goodbye to Berlin

Christopher Isherwood

Inspired by the author's own travels in 1930s Berlin, this short story collection captures the city's glamour, grit, and danger during Hitler's rise to power.

The Spy Who Came in from the Cold

John le Carré

A classic John le Carré spy novel that captures the reality of Cold War Berlin; the story follows a British intelligence officer as he embarks on his final mission across the Berlin Wall.

Another Country

Berlin has plenty of quirky bookshops, and this is one of the best of them. The checkerboard tiling and claret paintwork on the façade of Another Country are the first clues that something special awaits. Inside, more than 20,000 well-thumbed English-language classics and tattered tomes tumble from packed shelves, while rickety furniture and threadbare rugs make it feel more like an eccentric relative's home. Founded by local legend Sophie Raphaeline, who passed away in 2022, the shop has been lovingly kept afloat by a group of dedicated regulars. They run things just as Sophie did: books are priced fairly and you can return them after you've finished reading—you'll get your money back minus €1.50.

Riemannstraße 7, Kreuzberg; +49 30 69401160

Another Country

Jacob-und-Wilhelm-Grimm-Zentrum

Founded in 1809, the Humboldt-Universität is Berlin's oldest university. It makes sense, then, that such an illustrious institution should be home to a library that embodies intellectual sharpness in its design. From the outside, the Jacob-und-Wilhelm-Grimm-Zentrum's cubic, concrete structure and slitted windows look harsh, even a little dystopian. Get past the austere bunker vibes, however, and you'll realize just how spectacular the space is. The central reading room is a cavernous, multi-tiered expanse, set beneath a massive skylight. Peering out across the void is a sight to behold: some of Berlin's brightest minds sit in deafening silence, all furrowed brows punctuated by the occasional yawn.

Geschwister-Scholl-Straße 1-3, Mitte; ub.hu-berlin.de

The Empty Library

Situated on the southern end of the leafy Unter den Linden boulevard and framed by impressive Baroque buildings, Bebelplatz looks like any grand old European square. But it hardly could be. On an overcast evening in May 1933, tens of thousands of people listened to Joseph Goebbels (chief propagandist for the Nazi Party) preach hate here. Soon after, student members of the nationalist German Student Association marched in with burning torches and set fire to around 20,000 books, including works from famous German thinkers Karl Marx, Albert Einstein, and Heinrich Mann. Today, a solitary window in the center of the square looks down into an underground room lined with empty white bookshelves. The books may be gone, but their memory lives on here.

Bebelplatz 1, Mitte; visitberlin.de

Staatsbibliothek Potsdamer Straße

Staatsbibliothek Potsdamer Straße

It's a real fight for first place when it comes to Berlin's best libraries. Opened in 1978 with a striking Modernist design, the free-to-access Staatsbibliothek Potsdamer Straße is instantly eye-catching. Its golden-clad roof looks like an enormous ingot suspended in the sky, while its interior features breezy atriums, huge circular lights, and floor-to-ceiling windows. Sounds cinematic, right? Director Wim Wenders certainly thought so; spot the library in his 1987 classic, *Wings of Desire*.

Potsdamer Straße 33, Mitte; staatsbibliothek-berlin.de

Philological Library

Located in the suburb of Dahlem, the "Berlin Brain"—a nickname it earned due to its cerebral appearance—is a silvery, sci-fi structure designed by British architect Norman Foster. After walking through the library's bright-orange entrance, you'll be immersed in spacey grays and whites, with four open-plan floors wrapped by undulating balconies that double as desks. The interior is enclosed by an inner membrane, softening the natural light that streams through rectangular openings, offering glimpses of the sky outside. Not a bad place for a mid-study-session daydream.

Habelschwerdter Allee 45, Dahlem; fu-berlin.de

Pro qm

Pro qm is Berlin to a T. Firstly, there's the oh-so-trendy interior: teal-colored shelves, pink book ladders, whitewashed floors. Everything here is carefully curated, even down to the neat stacks of magazines on the steps leading to the shop's mezzanine. Then there's the effortlessly cool collection of art and design books that take center stage on the shelves. And finally, the events: this proudly interdisciplinary shop hosts regular talks on themes such as pop culture, architecture, urban planning, politics, and economic critique. Cerebral and highly intellectual, it's the perfect place for a chin scratch and a ponder of the bigger picture, in true Berliner style.

☞ Almstadtstraße 48, Mitte; pro-qm.de

AUTHOR PROFILE

Christopher Isherwood

Nobody captured the unbridled hedonism of Babylon Berlin quite like Christopher Isherwood (1904–1986). Having arrived here in 1929, the Anglo-American set about chronicling his experiences as a gay man living through the Weimar Republic's twilight-years. His diaries formed the basis of *Goodbye to Berlin* (1939), a partly autobiographical novel that centers on Nollendorfkiez, the heart of Berlin's queer scene.

Pro qm

She Said

For the most part, modern Berlin is an inclusive place where people can live and love freely, and this bookstore is a shining example of that. Opened in 2020, She Said is dedicated to selling titles by female, queer, and marginalized voices—there's a particularly great section of feminist criticism. It also welcomes its community with a packed roster of events, quiet shopping hours for neurodiverse folk, and a cool pink-and-green interior. There's a coffee shop too, if you don't want to leave just yet. Perhaps it's little wonder, then, that the shop has become a landmark in Berlin's contemporary literary scene, and a safe space for all.

Kottbusser Damm 79, Neukölln; shesaid.de

Dussmann

Spread over five floors, this gargantuan bookstore feels more like a department store than a cute book nook, but don't let that put you off. A staple for Berlin's bibliophiles since 1997, Dussmann is a go-to for just about any literary work—the English-language section is incredibly well stocked, with immaculate copies spanning all the major literary genres. After a good browse, the café, which sits underneath a huge vertical garden, is an impressive place to talk books over a coffee or two. If you prefer a bit of solitude, comfy brown leather sofas are scattered across the floors, perfectly positioned for melting into with a couple of potential picks, or for enjoying a bit of people-watching. As an added bonus, Dussmann is open until midnight on weekdays—ideal if you're a night owl (or in need of a very last-minute bookish present).

Friedrichstraße 90, Mitte; kulturkaufhaus.de

She Said

St. George's

Since 2003, the two brothers behind St. George's have been amassing the capital's largest selection of new and used English-language titles. That alone is worth shouting about, but there's more to St. George's than good stock. Tucked away on a cobblestoned street in the picturesque Prenzlauer Berg district, this is a neighborhood bookstore through and through. Many who pop by are regulars (staff greet them like the friends they are), books are chosen based on local tastes, and if they don't have what you're looking for, staff will order it in quick as a flash.

Wörther Straße 27, Prenzlauer Berg; saintgeorgesbookshop.com

German National Library

Leipzig

GERMANY | EUROPE

Known as Germany's "City of Books," Leipzig has been a center of literature for centuries. Today, it's most famous for its annual spring book fair, but there are plenty of other activities to tantalize book lovers year-round.

Leipzig's literary history stretches back centuries. This cool little city in the southeast state of Saxony has long been a hub for Germany's most popular publishers. It all began in 1650, when the world's first daily newspaper, *Einkommende Zeitungen*, was printed here. By the 18th century, Leipzig had grown into one of Europe's most important book-trade centers, its fairs drawing printers and scholars from across the continent. The University of Leipzig, where Goethe *(p. 153)* studied law in the 1760s, further bolstered the city's intellectual life—the German writer even immortalized a wine cellar here in his play *Faust*.

As the years went by, Leipzig only became more bookish. In the 19th and 20th centuries, the city dominated Germany's publishing industry; by the 1920s, more than 500 publishing houses operated in the city. Despite falling under the Communist East German (GDR) state after World War II, literary Leipzig continued to champion independent thought—writers' circles operated underground and intellectual resistance simmered beneath the surface. The city remains fiercely literary today: historic museums and bustling publishing houses line the streets, while the bigwigs of the book world stream in for the world-famous Leipzig Book Fair every year.

GETTING AROUND

Most of Leipzig's literary landmarks are within a 15-minute walk (or short cycle) of each other in the city center; an extensive tram network makes reaching other parts of the city straightforward.

READING LIST

Naked Among Wolves

Bruno Apitz

Written by Leipzig-born Apitz, who survived the Buchenwald concentration camp, this novel tells the story of World War II prisoners who risk their lives to protect a young child.

While We Were Dreaming

Clemens Meyer

Clemens Meyer's acclaimed debut novel (it was long-listed for the prestigious International Booker Prize in 2023) follows a group of young men coming of age in post-reunification Leipzig.

Love in Five Acts

Daniela Krien

Told through five interconnected stories, this novel traces the emotional lives of women living in contemporary Leipzig, exploring themes of love, loss, and resilience.

German National Library

Leipzig's branch of the national library is huge. There are multiple reading rooms, endless archives of historical documents and multimedia, and a fascinating museum: the German Museum of Books and Writing. The latter sits in an ultra-modern annex of the library, though it was actually founded in 1884 (making it the world's oldest museum of book culture)—its former location was destroyed in World War II and some of the exhibits still show signs of gunfire. You'll need a card to access the library's reading rooms (this is primarily a reference library, after all), but the museum is free. The permanent exhibition is dedicated to 5,000 years of media history, covering the pursuit of knowledge, the future of publishing, and censorship. There's a particularly great hands-on section dedicated to younger visitors, where kids can learn about paper production, hieroglyphs, and bookbinding techniques.

Deutscher Platz 1, Zentrum-Süd; dnb.de

Antiquariat an der Nikolaikirche

Set in the shadows of Leipzig's gorgeous St. Nicholas Church—its pink-and-mint nave worthy of a Wes Anderson film—this 30-year-old rare bookstore is home to thousands of elegantly yellowing tomes. It's a lovely place to explore, with ladders balancing against the floor-to-ceiling bookshelves and plenty of cozy nooks and crannies to hide away in as you browse. The owner, André Brauer, is a true bibliophile, the kind of person you *want* to run a bookstore. Having once nabbed a first edition (in German) of Bram Stoker's *Dracula*, he spent nights unable to sleep in sheer excitement; he's also got a particularly vast collection of books from the GDR era, a tumultuous but important time in Leipzig's history.

Ritterstraße 8-10, Mitte; antiquariat-brauer.de

Rotorbooks

Want to know where Leipzig's cool literary kids hang out? It's here. Located in the elegant Kolonnadenviertel neighborhood, to the west of the city center, Rotorbooks is a bustling independent bookstore. It specializes in literature that pushes boundaries—political philosophy, cultural and gender studies, contemporary art criticism, and the like—and draws in a steady stream of students and alternative folk, who mine the shelves for suitably intellectual titles and sip on the shop's excellent coffee. Throughout the year, the shop hosts a series of popular readings, discussions, and collaborations with local literary projects. There's no denying this is a stalwart of Leipzig's literary scene.

Kolonnadenstraße 5–7, Kolonnadenviertel; rotorbooks.de

Schillerhaus

Leipzig's Gohlis neighborhood is known for its swathe of gorgeous buildings and leafy green spaces. It's a suitably quaint setting for Friedrich Schiller's small farmhouse, where one of Germany's most celebrated playwrights and poets spent a heady summer writing. It's here he composed the historical tragedy *Don Carlo* and wrote a draft of his most famous poem, "Ode to Joy," in 1785. The house itself dates back to 1717 and is modest in size; you won't need too long to explore the space, but it's well worth wandering about the creaky floor plans and gazing upon period furnishings and Schiller-themed exhibits. It's all so charming, and, arguably, a more personal counterpoint to Leipzig's larger literary landmarks. Note that the house is closed between November and February.

Menckestraße 42, Gohlis; stadtgeschichtliches-museum-leipzig.de/besuch/unsere-haeuser/schillerhaus

Auerbachs Keller

Auerbachs Keller is one of Leipzig's oldest wine cellars. But what makes it bookish, you ask? Founded in 1525 by the physician Heinrich Stromer, it was once a gathering place for merchants, students, and writers, who drank and debated beneath its arched ceiling. Goethe immortalized the cellar in Part I of *Faust*, and today, visitors can gaze upon its vaulted rooms, adorned with murals depicting scenes from the drama, while enjoying some traditional Saxon dishes—the roasted wild boar is a favorite. Operating as both restaurant and monument, Auerbachs Keller offers a tangible link between literature and daily life, and that's something to raise a glass to.

☞ Grimmaische Straße 2-4, Mitte;
auerbachs-keller-leipzig.de

BOOK AT BEDTIME

Book Hotel Leipzig

Leipzig's Book Hotel *(book-hotel-leipzig.de)* embraces the city's literary spirit with packed shelves (borrow any book), reading nooks, literary-themed decor, and a range of bookish events. It's also within easy reach of Leipzig's literary landmarks.

Auerbachs Keller

Duchess Anna Amalia Library

Weimar

GERMANY | EUROPE

Weimar may be little, but it punches way above its weight when it comes to cultural legacy. Meet the birthplace of the groundbreaking Bauhaus school and the center of the famed literary movement Weimar Classical.

It's no exaggeration to say that Weimar changed German literature forever—though you might not expect it. Tucked away in central Germany amid rolling hills and farmers' fields, the city isn't often at the top of travelers' bucket lists. Learn a little about its history, however, and it soon will be. A place of cobbled streets, UNESCO-listed landmarks and intellectual fervor, Weimar first flourished in the 18th century, under the patronage of the Duchess Anna Amalia and her son, Duke Karl August. The pair transformed the city into a hub of creativity, and writers and artists soon moved in. One such intellect was Johann Wolfgang von Goethe, whose arrival in 1775 signaled the emergence of Weimar as the heart of German Classicism, a literary movement that promoted humanist ideals. Fellow intellect Friedrich Schiller came here in 1799 and together the pair came to define the principles of Weimar Classicism.

For more than two centuries, visitors have repeatedly been drawn to this legacy. Franz Kafka traveled to the city in 1912 to honor his literary hero, Goethe, while Thomas Mann immortalized Weimar in his 1939 novel, *Lotte in Weimar: The Beloved Returns*. And today, visitors still arrive in search of the same intellectual air.

GETTING AROUND

From Weimar's train station, a 20-minute downhill walk or a 10-minute bus ride leads to the historic old town, where most major sights lie within easy walking distance.

READING LIST

The Sorrows of Young Werther

Johann Wolfgang Goethe

This epistolary novel is set in the fictional village of Wahlheim and the (very real) city of Weimar. It was Goethe's first novel and made him an instant literary sensation.

Lotte in Weimar: The Beloved Returns

Thomas Mann

Mann's fictional story about his literary hero, Goethe, focuses, primarily on his romantic interest Charlotte Kestner (Lotte)—the woman who inspired *The Sorrows of Young Werther.*

Weimar

Katja Hoyer

German-British historian Katja Hoyer chronicles the rise and reign of Hitler through a cast of ordinary Weimar residents.

Duchess Anna Amalia Library

Often on the shortlist for most beautiful libraries in the world, this gorgeous bookish building was founded in 1766, at the behest of Duchess Anna Amalia. Its most swoon-worthy room is the oval white-and-gold Rococo Hall, which features three floors of curved bookcases and an ornately embellished ceiling. (Be sure to book a tour of the hall in advance, as visitor numbers are strictly limited.) Yet the Duchess Anna Amalia Library is more than just a pretty face. Goethe served as the library's director for 35 years, shaping its development and reputation. Today, it's both a public research library and a UNESCO World Heritage site, housing an exceptional collection of manuscripts and late-Romantic and Classical European literature (1750–1850). Visitors can also explore personal collections belonging to figures such as composer Franz Liszt and philosopher Friedrich Nietzsche.

Platz der Demokratie 1, Zentrum; klassik-stiftung.de/en/herzogin-anna-amalia-bibliothek

Café Fama

When Weimar's literary lovers aren't swooning in the Duchess Anna Amalia Library or browsing the city's bookstores, they're probably discussing their latest reads here. This relaxed, Scandinavian-style vegetarian café is a hit among the city's young, hip crowd, and not just for the delicious food (think homemade cakes and organic breakfasts). Café Fama hosts a number of well-maintained book-swap shelves—you're welcome to swap one of your own in or simply borrow a novel for a couple of hours as you sip on a lavender latte. The staff are easy going and are happy to let you linger.

Windischenstraße 20, Zentrum; +49 3643 9088786

Schiller Museum

Goethe played a decisive role in bringing Friedrich Schiller to Weimar in 1799. Recognizing his intellectual brilliance, he encouraged the playwright and poet to settle in the city—an arrival that firmly established Weimar as the center of German Classicism. The grand, marigold-colored Schiller Museum is the house where Schiller lived with his family during the final three years of his life, until his death in 1805. Here, under Goethe's encouragement to return to drama, Schiller wrote *William Tell* and *The Bride of Messina*. Take a peek into his study to see his original desk; you can also see the room in which he died at the age of 45 of tuberculosis. The museum's interactive studio offers a tactile reminder of literary labor, inviting visitors to try writing with a quill themselves.

Schillerstraße 12, Zentrum; klassik-stiftung.de/en/schiller-museum

Eckermann Buchhandlung

Tucked behind Weimar's market square is the cozy, half-timbered Eckermann Buchhandlung, a beloved local bookstore, known for its impressive international selection. It's a real stalwart of Weimar's literary scene: come here for readings by contemporary authors, book-themed brunches, art exhibitions, or traditional celebrations of Goethe. Its location is fitting, too: the building was once home to Johann Peter Eckermann, Goethe's close friend and personal secretary. Eckermann is best known for his work *Conversations with Goethe*, a record of dialogues that chronicle the final nine years of the writer's life—making this bookstore, you could say, a living extension of Weimar's literary past.

Marktstraße 2, Zentrum; eckermannbuchhandlung.buchhandlung.de

Goethehaus

Goethehaus

Goethe's daily commute was brief: his two-story Baroque townhouse is a stone's throw from the Duchess Anna Amalia Library. He lived here for nearly 50 years, and it was within these ornate walls that he worked on his iconic tragic play, *Faust*. A passionate collector, Goethe also amassed some 26,000 artworks and 23,000 natural-science specimens, a selection of which is displayed across the 18 rooms open to curious visitors. Goethe's first residence in Weimar lies just a 10-minute walk away: the smaller yet equally regal Gartenhaus was where Goethe wrote *Erlkönig*, his most famous ballad.

Frauenplan 1, Zentrum; klassik-stiftung.de

AUTHOR PROFILE

Johann Wolfgang von Goethe

Germany's most influential writer, Goethe moved to Weimar in 1775 and lived there until his death in 1832. He originally trained as a lawyer in Leipzig *(p. 147)*, but soon broadened his scope; a prolific polymath, his complete works span more than 140 volumes, encompassing literature, science, and philosophy. He is often considered equivalent to Shakespeare in terms of literary influence.

The Black Diamond

Copenhagen

DENMARK | EUROPE

With its colorful houses, cobbled streets, and historic spires, bijou Copenhagen is like a scene from a picture book. No wonder, then, that it's long been an inspiring place for literary lovers, especially those with a penchant for fairy tales.

Walk through Copenhagen's historic streets and you could be forgiven for thinking you've fallen into one of Hans Christian Andersen's stories. Palace guards dressed like his tin soldiers march around the royal buildings. Ugly ducklings glide through the harbor where a little mermaid sits and wistfully surveys the rocks. And colorful peacocks strut through Tivoli Gardens theme park, which inspired Andersen to create the world of "The Nightingale." Born in Odense, the master storyteller lived and wrote in the Danish capital, and his spirit lives on today.

Copenhagen might be a small city, but it's had an outsize impact on the writing world: from *Out of Africa* author (and exceptional short story writer) Karen Blixen to philosopher Søren Kierkegaard and memoirist Tove Ditlevsen, many of the city's authors have enjoyed worldwide success. And the tradition continues today, with contemporary Danish authors like Solvej Balle and Olga Ravn drawing in new readers.

It's perhaps little wonder that Copenhagen is the common denominator—and not just because of the fairy-tale vibes. This Scandi capital is, after all, famed for its design-led bookstores, uber-modern libraries, and world-class Louisiana Literature Festival. For book lovers, it's a dream.

GETTING AROUND

Copenhagen city center is easily tackled on foot, or do as the locals do and hop on a bike—distances are fairly short and bike lanes are plentiful. Outer areas can be reached via the public transit system.

READING LIST

Hans Christian Andersen's Fairy Tales

Rooted in 19th-century Copenhagen, Andersen's timeless tales blend whimsy, melancholy, and moral insight, reflecting the city's streets, canals, and social life.

The Copenhagen Trilogy

Tove Ditlevsen

A semiautobiographical exploration of childhood, adolescence, and early adulthood in mid-20th-century Copenhagen, this trilogy captures the city's working-class neighborhoods alongside the struggles and inner life of its narrator.

The Danish Girl

David Ebershoff

This historical novel traces the life of Danish painter Lili Elbe, one of the first people in the world to undergo gender-affirming surgery.

The Old Reading Room, the Black Diamond

The Black Diamond, Royal Danish Library

A slab of dark reflective glass overlooking the water, the Black Diamond is attached to the older Royal Danish Library, built in 1906. It's a clever reworking of what a library can be, adding important social and community elements to the established building, which includes all works printed in Denmark since the 17th century. Join college students in the high-ceilinged reading room and tourists browsing the exhibition spaces, or drop by for events with international authors.

☞ Søren Kierkegaards Pl. 1, Indre By; kb.dk/en/visit-us/black-diamond-copenhagen

Paludan Book Café

A warren of book-lined passages greets you at one of the city's oldest literary cafés. Since it opened in 1895, this café and antiquarian bookstore has welcomed bibliophiles and students in particular, located as it is around the corner from Copenhagen University. Home to a series of bookcase-bordered rooms, many of which are filled with brown hardbacks with gilded titles, it has an old-fashioned library-like air to it, complete with low-level lighting and oil paintings on the walls. In the basement, well-thumbed secondhand books in Danish, English and various other languages are on sale for a handful of coins.

☞ Fiolstræde 10, Indre By; paludanbogcafe.com

Library Bar

Copenhagen's bar scene is dominated by sleek designer bars with clean lines and elegant cocktails, but this place is different. With the style and flair of a gentleman's club (think low lighting, oxblood Chesterfields, and wood-paneled walls), the historic Library Bar is a step back into another time. First editions and leather-bound books line the walls, while the cocktail list takes inspiration from literary classics with names such as Grapes of Wrath, Norwegian Wood, and Beowulf, the latter set not so far away in Lejre. As they put it, every sip tells a story. On Friday and Saturday nights, the bar turns into an intimate jazz club, drawing on Copenhagen's history as one of Europe's historic hubs for this foot-tapping music genre.

☞ Bernstorffsgade 4, Vesterbro; ligula.se/da/the-library-bar

Karen Blixen's House

Assistens Churchyard

Graveyards are not considered solemn in Denmark, something seen at Assistens Churchyard, a pocket of leafy green to the west of the center where people come to stroll, cycle, and picnic. Established during the mid-18th century, this cemetery is where some of the country's best and brightest are buried, among them Hans Christian Andersen, famed writer of fairy tales. His simple gravestone, which rises up between two hedges, is fronted by colorful flowers. There are plenty of other sights in the city that honor Andersen, including his statue in the manicured King's Garden; the red-fronted house at Nyhavn 20, where he lived when he had his first fairy tales published; and *The Little Mermaid* sculpture, an ode to one of his most beloved tales.

☞ Kapelvej 2, Nørrebro; kk.dk/brug-byen/natur-og-groenne-omraader/koebenhavns-kirkegaarde

Karen Blixen's House

Around 40 minutes by train from Copenhagen Central Station, a trip to captivating Rungstedlund, the former home of author Karen Blixen, is an essential stop for her fans. The country house, surrounded by bird-rich gardens, contains an excellent museum of her life and work. Courage, humor, and love were her guiding forces in life and shape the museum's approach. Walk through her beautiful old house and read panels in Danish and English about her tragic love life—the love of her life, British aristocrat Denys Finch Hatton, died in a plane crash in Africa—and her glittering literary life. Discover kitchens inspired by her short story "Babette's Feast," and a room dedicated to the 17 years she spent in Kenya, the inspiration for her most famous work, *Out of Africa*. At the lovely café, you can enjoy a Baroness brunch in her honor.

☞ Rungsted Strandvej, Rungsted; blixen.dk

FESTIVAL

Louisiana Literature Festival

For three days every August, Denmark's most beloved contemporary art gallery opens its lawns and halls to some of the world's finest writers, hosting readings, performances, and discussions.

Books & Company

Copenhagen University Library

On a street in the heart of the historic old town sits Copenhagen University's grand library, a decorated red-brick building that dates to 1861. After serious renovations, it was fully restored and opened to the general public in 2023, but it remains a bit of a hidden secret. It's a delightful bookish sight to discover, from its stained-glass windows and painted ceiling to its laden bookshelves hung with movable book ladders. It's no exaggeration to say that browsing its age-old shelves makes you feel like you're in the restricted section of the library at Hogwarts. There are some oddities to discover too, including a cabinet of curiosities from the city's Medical Museum. Take a tour—included in the entry fee—to discover the medieval history behind the library and its dungeon-like cellar.

Fiolstræde 1, Indre By; kub.ku.dk/english/fiolstraede

Books & Company

Tucked away on a side street in chichi Hellerup, this English bookstore is the epicenter of English-language literary life in Copenhagen, hosting numerous author talks, book clubs, and writing clubs. There's so much for literature lovers here: peruse its stand of glossy global magazines, from *Monocle* to *Condé Nast Traveler*; browse its bookshelves packed with great reads; and admire the eye-catching window display, sometimes themed by cover color. Don't miss out on ordering a coffee, either, and shooting the literary breeze with the owner, Isabella, or one of her well-read and knowledgeable staff. And if you're visiting with older children? Head here on the weekends, when the kids' section is often staffed by volunteer teenagers, who share personal recommendations on the best YA fiction.

Sofievej 1, Hellerup; booksandcompany.dk

Copenhagen University Library

Kronborg Castle

Hamlet's Kronborg

DENMARK | EUROPE

The setting for the Bard's iconic tragic play Hamlet, *Kronborg Castle's spires and stone courtyards play host to literary ghosts and an annual Shakespeare festival. It's a spine-tingling place to visit for anyone with a passing knowledge of the play. As you walk its restored halls, it's easy to imagine intrigue behind tapestry wall hangings and nobles carousing in the grand, checkerboard-floored ballroom.*

Shakespeare's Birthplace, Stratford-upon-Avon

The place where it all began: visit the Bard's birthplace, his wife Anne Hathaway's cottage, and, of course, the Royal Shakespeare Theatre; the latter is dedicated to his works and is home to the Royal Shakespeare Company.

shakespeare.org.uk

Iona Abbey, Iona

The ancient monastery of Iona, located on a tiny island off the Scottish Isle of Mull, is the evocative final resting place for the real-life Duncan and Macbeth, who appear in *Macbeth*.

historicenvironment.scot

Rialto Bridge, Venice

The Merchant of Venice comes alive in this Italian city. Head to the center of commerce in the play to ask, like its characters, "What news on the Rialto?"

italia.it

The Tower of London, London

The final indignity for Richard II, in Shakespeare's play of the same name, sees the king thrown in a cell in the Tower of London, where he soliloquizes about his sorry lot.

hrp.org.uk/tower-of-london

Its gilded spires and turrets looming above the icy Øresund Sound, this UNESCO-listed Renaissance castle has a formidable air to it. Fitting, given it was the inspiration for Shakespeare's ghoulish Elsinore Castle, the setting of *Hamlet*. While the Bard never actually visited this coastal fort, historical evidence shows that three actors from his company, the Lord Chamberlain's Men, spent a season performing plays for the Danish king here (just before *Hamlet* was written). Their tales of the windswept building greatly inspired the playwright.

Today, visitors can discover the battlements where the guards spy the ghost of Hamlet's father, and the evocative narrow hallways where our hero monologues to excess. Best of all is the summer Shakespeare Festival, where visiting companies perform on a stage that rises up from the castle moat.

William Shakespeare

Strahov Monastery Library

Prague

CZECH REPUBLIC | EUROPE

Lose yourself amid Prague's ancient, labyrinthine lanes and centuries-old buildings to discover a city that has inspired the imaginations of writers from around the world.

Prague's soaring Gothic spires and dark, cobblestone alleyways have proven uncommonly fertile ground for world literature. In the early 20th century, the Czech capital gave us Franz Kafka, who played on Prague's medieval cityscape to cook up haunting phantasmagoria like *The Trial* and *The Castle*. Around the same time, local satirist Jaroslav Hašek lampooned the empire through his *The Good Soldier Švejk*, the tale of a bumbling soldier who marches through the waste and folly of World War I. In the decades under Communism, the Czechs' own favorite writer, Bohumil Hrabal, transformed the city's everyday settings (its pubs, hotels, and train stations) into tender tragicomedy. And when the Communist regime finally collapsed, the country cemented its literary street cred by elevating Václav Havel, a playwright, to the role of president.

Now a UNESCO City of Literature, Prague rewards book lovers with its fascinating literary history and host of bookish haunts. Libraries and literary cafés here are lavish and legendary, while thriving local bookstores are found within buildings little changed since the days of Kafka et al.

GETTING AROUND

Metros and trams are excellent and affordable, zipping travelers to just about anywhere in Prague. Many of the city's central districts (such as the Old Town) are easily walkable.

READING LIST

The Good Soldier Švejk

Jaroslav Hašek

Hysterically funny in spots, Hašek's wry, witty tale of a bumbling soldier is aimed at the Austro-Hungarian monarchy and the tragic folly of World War I.

The Unbearable Lightness of Being

Milan Kundera

Kundera's most famous work is a masterful philosophical novel which chronicles the period of the Prague Spring protests.

The Trial

Franz Kafka

Prague may rarely be named in Kafka's work, but you'll sense its presence lurking in many of his books. *The Trial*, which follows a man accused of a crime he didn't commit, is one of the writer's most famous.

The view from Klementinum's Astronomical Tower

Strahov Monastery Library

Perched on a leafy hillside near Prague Castle, the 12th-century Strahov Monastery houses two magnificent reading halls that, taken together, regularly make it onto lists of the world's most beautiful libraries. First up is the Theological Hall: built in the 1670s, it glimmers with Baroque stucco and ceiling frescoes inspired by the Book of Proverbs. Next, there's the even grander Philosophical Hall. Completed in the 1790s, it features elegant, decorative bookcases beneath another magnificent ceiling fresco. Together, the halls hold some 200,000 volumes, but really you're here to stop, stare, and say, "Wow."

Strahovské nádvoří 1/132, Hradčany; strahovskyklaster.cz

Klementinum

Choose your fighter: Strahov or Klementinum. Home to another grand reading hall, Prague's second-largest building complex began life as a 16th-century Jesuit college. Today it houses the still-active Czech National Library and its swoon-worthy Library Hall. This softly lit treasure of frescoed ceilings, gilded woodwork, antique globes, and more than 20,000 whitened-spine theological tomes is a Baroque beauty. It's also one of protagonist Robert Langdon's favorite spots in Dan Brown's *The Secret of Secrets*. After standing in awe of the library, climb up the building's soaring Astronomical Tower—it offers sweeping views over the Old Town.

Klementinum 190, Staré Město; prague.eu

Central Library

Visitors line up at the door of this Art Deco building for one thing and one thing only: *IDIOM*. The work of Slovak artist Matej Krén, this thought-provoking art installation (or perhaps better, optical illusion) stands in the library's vestibule. It's also called the *Column of Knowledge*, perhaps a more fitting name for this cylindrical tower forged from around 8,000 stacked books. Peer through a teardrop-shaped opening along its side, and mirrors positioned at the top and bottom create a dizzying illusion of infinite depth. *IDIOM* has been standing here since 1998, but the growth of the internet has transformed it into something of a social-media phenomenon. What's beyond the book tower? The library also hosts an array of cultural events, from lectures to concerts, and features a number of cozy study spaces.

☞ Mariánské náměstí 98/1, Staré Město; mlp.cz

IDIOM, Prague Central Library

Shakespeare & Sons

This bookish hideaway is set along a cobbled lane, just around the corner from Prague's iconic Charles Bridge. Its inviting space is chock-a-block with books; there are some 20,000 titles squeezed in here, making Shakespeare & Sons Prague's largest independent English-language bookstore. The street-level space bustles with browsers scanning tomes of fiction, poetry, and travel, while the vaulted basement—which looks out over an atmospheric stream of the Vltava River—hosts regular readings, open-mic nights, and local art exhibitions. As with any good bookstore, the staff at Shakespeare & Sons are passionate readers themselves and happy to steer you toward some Czech literature in translation.

☞ U Lužického semináře 10, Malá Strana; shakes.cz

Globe Bookstore & Café

In 1993—in the aftermath of the Velvet Revolution that overthrew the old Communist regime—five young Americans opened one of Prague's earliest English-language bookstores. Back then, the Globe was housed in a ramshackle space within the industrial Holešovice district. But as word spread of this literary hub, and more folks passed through its doors—a mix of Czech and international writers, as well as a scruffier coterie of expats, backpackers, and wannabe poets—the Globe soon upgraded. You'll now find it in a handsome Neo-Classical building located in Prague's New Town district. It's a lovely, moody-red space, hosting a lively café and restaurant that serves American brunch during the day, and hosts an array of events come evening (literary readings, bar trivia, live music, and poetry). Despite the changes, the Globe's roots remain the same: there are some 10,000 English-language books here, with a particularly strong Central European fiction section.

☞ Pštrossova 6, Nové Město; globebookstore.cz

Café Slavia

Taking a nod from 19th-century Vienna *(p.134)*, a city particularly famed for linking coffee and literary culture, Café Slavia has stimulated generations of legendary writers since opening in 1884. The Prague-born German poet Rainer Maria Rilke was an early regular. Between the world wars, writers like Karel Čapek (who coined the word "robot") and Nobel laureate Jaroslav Seifert held court here, too. Later, during the Communist occupation in the 1970s and 1980s, the playwright Václav Havel claimed his favorite window table and penned essays like *The Power of the Powerless*. Stop by in the evening for a glass of wine, or savor a coffee during the day like the literary greats before you.

☞ Smetanovo nábřeží 1012/2, Staré Město; cafeslavia.cz

Franz Kafka Museum

Perhaps no writer is more synonymous with a city than Franz Kafka is with Prague, and this immersive museum in the Malá Strana district is all about connecting writer to place. The permanent exhibition "The City of K" features original letters, photographs, manuscripts, diaries, and audio-visual installations, showing visitors both how Prague shaped Kafka's fiction and how his fiction reimagined Prague as a cauldron of dark comedy and alienation. There are plenty more Kafka-themed sites around Prague (ideal for a walking tour); just outside the city center you'll also find his modest, Cubist grave-marker in the New Jewish Cemetery.

☞ Cihelná 2b, Malá Strana, Prague 1; kafkamuseum.cz

Café Slavia

Franz Kafka's Prague

Born and raised in Prague, Kafka spent most of his life wandering the narrow alleyways of the Old Town and former Jewish Quarter. This route traces points along the author's journey that helped shape his world view and feed his unorthodox and innovative imagination.

i

DISTANCE
1.5 miles (2 km)

WALKING TIME
Allow an hour

NEAREST TRANSIT
Staroměstská, on metro line A, is the station closest to the start

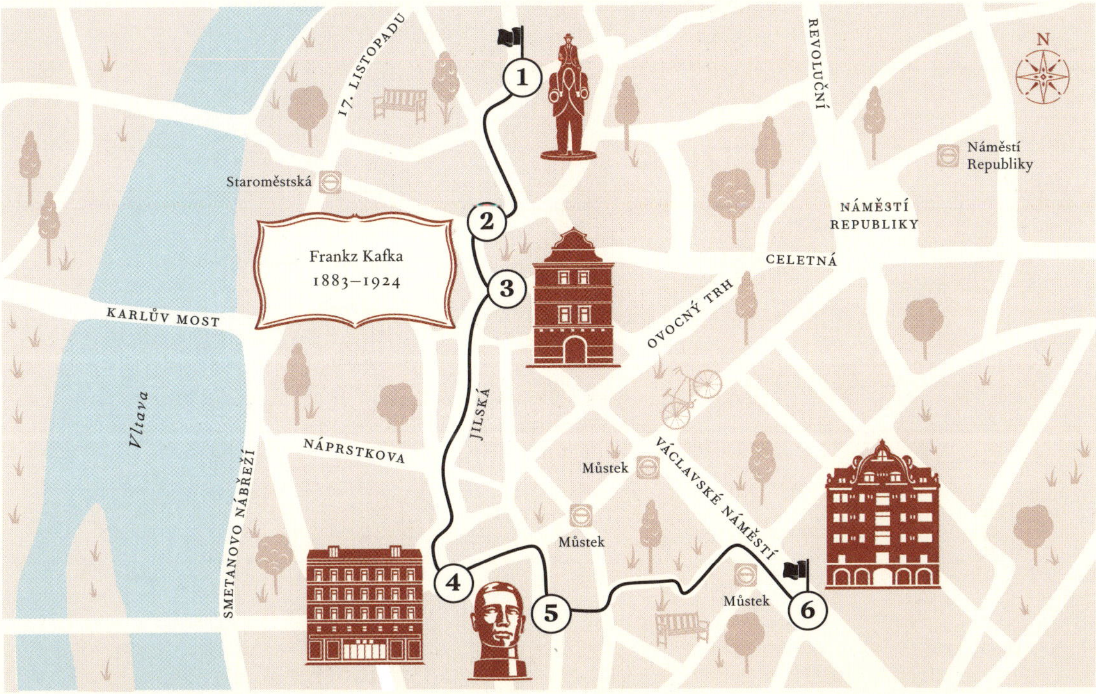

1. Franz Kafka Monument

Czech sculptor Jaroslav Róna's haunting statue depicts Kafka sitting atop an empty suit, an image adapted from the author's 1904 short story "Description of a Struggle" *(corner of Dušní and Široka)*.

2. Kafka's Birthplace

A plaque marks the site, just on the border between the Old Town and former Jewish Quarter, where Kafka was born in 1883. The original building burned down in 1887 *(Nám Franze Kafky 18/6)*.

3. House at the Minute

The Kafka family lived in this opulent Renaissance building from 1889 to 1896, during Kafka's preteen years. It's now owned by Prague municipality *(Staroměstské nám 3/2)*.

4. Café Louvre

Kafka was a regular at this grand, Neo-Rococo café around the turn of the 20th century, when it functioned as the de facto center for German-speaking writers and intellectuals *(Národní 22)*.

5. Franz Kafka—Rotating Head

This fascinating kinetic sculpture, by Czech installation artist David Černý, depicts Kafka's fragmented face as 42 layered, moving panels *(Charvátova)*.

6. W Prague

This Art Nouveau hotel was the setting for Kafka's only known public reading, in 1912. The writer recited from his short story, "The Judgment" *(Vaclavske namesti 826/25)*.

Sahaflar Çarşısı

Istanbul

TURKEY | EUROPE/ASIA

Straddling two ancient continents, Istanbul has snared countless writers over the years with its mesmerizing energy. Books aren't just found in ordinary bookstores here: rifle through crowded bazaars or browse the shelves of repurposed pier buildings.

Split by the mighty Bosporus Strait, Istanbul has a unique position at the cultural confluence between East and West. This coming together of worlds is evident everywhere, from the ancient architecture sharing space with contemporary cultural sights to the din of busy bars competing with the muezzin's meditative call to prayer. There's a sense of faded glory here, too; it's a living, breathing monument to the great empires of old. But beyond the patchwork history, there's something much deeper at play. It's hard to put your finger on it at first, but it's here: a heavy atmosphere that's nostalgic yet sorrowful. This anguish has a name in Turkish—*hüzün*—a profound melancholy that's deeply rooted in Istanbul's collective psyche. It's a longing that's influenced the work of several writers down the ages, from classic authors like Ahmet Hamdi Tanpınar to contemporary novelists like Orhan Pamuk and Elif Şafak.

Powerful stuff, and you can sample it, too. Whether you're tumbling in and out of dusty book nooks, exploring well-curated museums dedicated to Turkish literature, or bartering with enterprising hawkers in winding markets, Istanbul will leave an indelible mark on your imagination.

GETTING AROUND

Even though Istanbul is vast, areas like Beyoğlu, Galata, and Fatih are walkable (albeit a bit steep). The public transportation network is great (trams, buses, a metro line), while breezy ferries offer stunning views.

READING LIST

My Name Is Red

Orhan Pamuk

Orhan Pamuk's award-winning philosophical murder mystery delves into the lives of miniaturists living in Istanbul during the Ottoman Empire.

A Mind at Peace

Ahmet Hamdi Tanpınar

This lyrical homage to Istanbul follows Mümtaz, a young intellectual, as he wanders the city reflecting on love, tradition, and modernity, just before the outbreak of World War II.

10 Minutes 28 Seconds in This Strange World

Elif Şafak

After sex worker Tequila Leila is murdered in Istanbul, her consciousness reflects on her life. Şafak's unflinching novel was shortlisted for the Booker Prize in 2019.

Ahmet Hamdi Tanpınar Edebiyat Müze Kütüphanesi

Ahmet Hamdi Tanpınar (1901–1962) is one of Turkey's most celebrated authors: during his life, he penned numerous poems, essays, and novels. This little museum (which squeezes in some 9,000 exhibits) is dedicated to him and numerous other Turkish writers. It's housed in a 16th-century parade kiosk, built into the walls of Gülhane Park at Topkapı Palace. Wandering through its highly stylized interior (among polished floors and painted frescoes), it's no stretch of the imagination to picture Ottoman sultans sitting beside the stained-glass windows, awaiting the salute of janissaries parading below.

Gülhane Parkı içi 1, Fatih; ahtem.kutuphane.gov.tr

Sahaflar Çarşısı

Istanbul is ancient, and you'll certainly feel it in Fatih, with its winding alleyways and historic landmarks (like the hulking Hagia Sophia mosque). The area is also home to Sahaflar Çarşısı, an open-air bookseller's market that's been in situ since the 15th century. Modernity seems to slip away as you pass under the stone archway at the bazaar's entrance and into an enticing courtyard of sun-dappled paths. Wooden stalls nestle together, while shrewd hawkers tempt you to playfully haggle over antique tomes—legend has it that they sell their wares to those most interested in the topic, not the highest bidder. Occasionally, you'll spot a blissed-out cat curled up inside a crate full of books. It's a lovely place to linger.

Çadırcılar Caddesi, Fatih

AUTHOR PROFILE

Orhan Pamuk

Few writers have captured Istanbul's allure as deftly as Orhan Pamuk. Pamuk was born here in 1952, and several of his books—including *My Name Is Red* (1998) and the largely autobiographical *Istanbul: Memories and the City* (2005)—reveal the deep-seated tension between Eastern and Western values that characterizes the city. Always wistful, his work was awarded the Nobel Prize in Literature in 2006.

Museum of Innocence

There's nowhere quite like this curious museum. Housed in a claret-colored townhouse, this is a real-world manifestation of Orhan Pamuk's novel, *Museum of Innocence*. The Nobel laureate began collecting the items displayed here in the mid-1990s, using them as the basis for his tale of unrequited love. Over a thousand objects, including pocket watches, gnarled cigarette butts, and photographs, are amassed (as the story goes) by the book's protagonist as artifacts of moments shared with his lover. It's haunting how the ephemera of daily life make Pamuk's characters so tangible. You don't need to have read the book before visiting, but it helps.

Çukurcuma Caddesi 2, Beyoğlu; masumiyetmuzesi.org

İstanbul Kitapçısı Karaköy

It's highly likely that you'll be using Istanbul's ferry network while you're here. So, what could be better than perusing a bookstore as you wait for the next departure? Tucked away inside Karaköy's pier, İstanbul Kitapçısı is suitably nautical: shelves are separated by gaping portholes that give you a sea-level view onto the topaz Bosporus. The terrace is a particularly scenic spot.

Rıhtım Caddesi 2, Karaköy; istanbulkitapcisi.com

Minoa Pera

Minoa Pera

Minoa Pera might just be Istanbul's favorite bookstore café. Housed in a grand old apartment building, it features a stunning Art Nouveau façade, but it's even better inside: all creeping plants, hanging lanterns, and winding staircases lined with books. Aesthetes flitter about, snapping photographs from all angles, while others weave between the shelves, arms piled ambitiously high with books—there are some 45,000 titles, in both Turkish and English, to choose from. You can watch it all from the second-floor café, where friends catch up and freelancers tap away on laptops.

☞ Meşrutiyet Caddesi 99, Beyoğlu; minoa.com

Salt Galata

From the outside, Salt Galata gives off an institutional vibe. It figures—the building, a fusion of Neo-Classical and Oriental architecture, was once the headquarters of the Imperial Ottoman Bank. Repurposed, yet keeping many original features, today it's home to a vibrant cultural center. It's all very impressive, particularly the atrium in the heart of the building. Here, sturdy Corinthian columns frame ornate balustrades from where you can peer down into the space where the bank's vault would have been. One giant safe remains, but like the rest of the center, it's now filled with books.

☞ Bankalar Caddesi 11, Karaköy; saltonline.org

Atatürk Cultural Center Library

Atatürk Cultural Center Library

Meet Istanbul's uber-contemporary cultural center. Located just off Taksim Square (often described as the city's modern heart), the Atatürk Cultural Center was originally opened in 1969; it was later rebuilt in 2021, and, boy, has it had a glow-up. Huge glass windows line the entrance; a massive, red-tiled sphere (you'll have to see it to believe it) leads to a yawning concert hall; and elegant, spiraling stairs transport visitors to the upper levels. Aside from the concert hall, there's a cinema, two art galleries, and, best of all, a stunning library. The latter specializes in music, arts, architecture, and design books, and while it's mainly used as a research space for students, it's still a gorgeous place to wander. Warm wood rules the design, creating a warm, relaxing atmosphere, and cozy reading spaces are carved out between the shelves, ideal for hunkering down with a gorgeous photo book.

Gümüşsuyu, Tak-ı Zafer Cd, Beyoğlu; test.akmistanbul.gov.tr/library

Akmar Passage (Kadıköy Sahafları)

A stone's throw from the Kadıköy neighborhood's ferry terminal, this treasure trove of secondhand books is spread across a two-story network of passageways, concealed beneath an unassuming office building. Navigating the corridors here can feel disorientating; endless rows of bookstores seem to go on infinitely, peddling everything from school textbooks to burly encyclopedias to long-forgotten classics. It's a bit like tumbling down a rabbit hole; there are no windows either, which adds to the subterranean feel. But for book lovers open to a little adventure, it's well worth exploring (just try to keep your bearings as you wander ...).

Akmar Pasajı, Mühürdar Caddesi 8/a, Kadıköy

Moda Pier Library

Moda Pier Library

If you're looking for some calm, go catch your breath in Moda. Tucked on the city's Anatolian flank, this charming neighborhood is beloved for its laid-back pace, and the pier's library is easily one of the area's most relaxing spots. Like many of the city's civic-owned jetties, Moda Pier was renovated in the 21st century in a bid to make it more community-oriented. Today, the building at the end of the pier is home to a modern book café, library, and working space, where locals sip cheap *çay* (tea), freelancers lock in—there's hardly a more scenic spot to work, given the sea-facing windows—and fishers natter outside.

Moda Caddesi 175, Kadıköy

El Fishawy Café

Cairo

EGYPT | AFRICA

Pick up any piece of local literature and Cairo's presence will be undeniable. The Egyptian capital is so historic, so atmospheric, so unabashedly loud that it nearly always becomes the main character—and writers can only bow to its power.

The sprawling, centuries-old Egyptian capital has a vivid presence in literature: read any good book set in Cairo and its scenery will sear into your imagination. There's the minaret-speckled, medieval core. The wide boulevards, trimmed by the faded architecture of Egypt's belle époque. The sinuous Nile. The dry desert hem, punctured by Giza's pyramids. This is a stage set for drama, and good authors know just how to use it.

Few writers have engaged with this cityscape quite like Naguib Mahfouz, the Arab world's most lauded writer. Much of the historic Gamaliya district, studded with madrassas and mosques, is still recognizable as the backdrop Mahfouz used in his famed *Cairo Trilogy* novels. During the early 20th century, European authors also wrote the city into their work, though the haunts of their privileged lifestyles—described in Michael Ondaatje's *The English Patient* and Olivia Manning's *The Levant Trilogy*—have mostly fallen into dilapidation.

Today it's the frenetic street life and symphonic din of a city bursting at its seams that provides a canvas for contemporary Egyptian writers, like Noor Naga. Browse the city's bookstores, packed with local and international literature, and you'll see that Cairo still calls to creatives. And they answer.

GETTING AROUND

Cairo's metro is useful for zipping between districts. Due to traffic, it's often quicker to walk than take a taxi when exploring particular neighborhoods, though crossing busy roads can prove challenging.

READING LIST

The Cairo Trilogy

Naguib Mahfouz

Set in early 20th-century Cairo, this epic trilogy follows a middle-class family across three generations, capturing a changing Egyptian society as it goes.

The Yacoubian Building

Alaa Al Aswany

Taking place in a once-grand apartment building in downtown Cairo, this novel interweaves the stories of its various residents. The building is real—spot it on Sharia Talaat Harb in Downtown.

Moon Tiger

Penelope Lively

Winner of the 1987 Booker Prize, *Moon Tiger* takes place in Cairo (among other places) around the time of World War II. It's a dazzling tale of devastating loss and heady desire.

Diwan Bookstore

Welcome to Egypt's first contemporary independent bookstore. Diwan has been Cairo's leading literary light since it was founded in 2002 by three Egyptian women. Swing open the door—off 26th of July Street's car-clogged hustle—and you'll enter a tranquil sanctuary devoted to books. Here, well-ordered shelves showcase the latest Arabic and English fiction and nonfiction, while the on-site café offers restorative coffee and cake. If this bookish bubble seems like a minor miracle amid Cairo's chaotic din, it's because it is; while there, buy a copy of *Chronicles of a Cairo Bookseller* by Diwan cofounder Nadia Wassef—it tells the tale of how, despite censorship, bureaucracy, and criticism, the founders made Diwan a Cairo institution.

☞ Sharia 26th of July, Zamalek; diwanegypt.com

Al-Azbakiyya Book Market

AUC Bookstore

Want to explore Egypt's surplus of temples and tombs? Head here first. Tucked into a corner of the American University in Cairo's (AUC's) Tahrir Square complex, this is a one-stop shop for all Egypt-related books. Its nonfiction selection is particularly good; this is, after all, the official bookshop for Cairo's AUC Press (the Middle East's leading English-language academic book publisher). Shelves sweep from Egyptology, Islamic architecture, and Coptic art to guidebooks, glossy coffee-table books, and travel memoirs. The clientele, meanwhile, are fittingly intellectual: expect to browse in the company of historical researchers, visiting archaeologists, and super-keen university students.

☞ Sharia El-Sheikh Rihan, Downtown; aucpress.com

Al-Azbakiyya Book Market

Al-Azbakiyya Book Market is a lucky-dip for literary lovers. Take a stroll and you might uncover a rare first edition hidden beneath some dusty classics, old newspapers, and secondhand books covering every topic from philosophy to engineering. This used book market has been part of Downtown's fabric since 1907, when booksellers set up makeshift stalls along the fence of Azbakiyya Gardens. According to market lore, Gamal Abdel Nasser (first president of Egypt) regularly hunted for books here during his student days, while in the mid-20th century, some of the biggest names in Arabic literature—including Naguib Mahfouz and Taha Hussein—could be found picking through the piles of tomes. Since then, the market has moved to a modern custom-built complex inside the gardens, giving Azbakiyya's 130-odd stalls a permanent home. Little else has changed though.

☞ Azbakeya Garden, Attaba, Downtown

Naguib Mahfouz Museum

Housed in a restored Ottoman-era building, this fascinating museum celebrates the life and work of Naguib Mahfouz (1911–2006), the Arab world's only Nobel Laureate in Literature. Visitors can discover an array of Mahfouz's personal effects, including his vast library and writing desk, along with rooms dedicated to his childhood, his 1987 Nobel Prize award, and the 1994 assassination attempt by fundamentalists, which temporarily thwarted his prolific output. One of the unexpected joys of a visit here is that the plot of Mahfouz's *Cairo Trilogy* (first published in Arabic throughout 1956–1957), unfurls only steps from the museum entrance, fully immersing you in his characters' world.

Sharia al-Tablita, Gamaliya; mahfouzmuseum.gov.eg

El Fishawy Café

Step inside this *ahwa* (traditional coffee house) and you'll be swept back in time. In business since 1797, this is one of Egypt's oldest—maybe *the* oldest—cafés. It's a world of clouded mirrors and dusty chandeliers, amid which locals catch up over *karkadai* (a cold hibiscus drink) or *shay nana* (tea with mint) and puff on shishas. Just the type of ambience to induce the inspiration (say) for a best-selling family saga set in the surrounding neighborhood; at least, that's what Naguib Mahfouz found. The writer was a regular customer at El Fishawy, and local legend claims *Palace Walk* (the first book in the series) was partially written at a table here. Grab a seat, sit back and enjoy the old-world atmosphere, which comes complete with ample interruptions from roving musicians and charismatic street hawkers.

Khan el-Khalili, Gamaliya

El Fishawy Café

Greater Cairo Public Library

Established in 1995, the Greater Cairo Public Library is the largest library in Egypt, and a go-to for Cairo's readers. The book collection is impressive, but the building might just be the highlight here. Built in 1902 as the Nile-side palace of Princess Samiha Kamil, it features a sweeping grand staircase that leads to salons and halls resplendent with Andalusian, Moroccan, and Ottoman decorative flourishes, and now full of shelves of books. Be sure to check out the garden, too; it's home to a lovely café on the banks of the Nile.

17 Sharia Mohammed Mazhar, Zamalek; +20 2 27362271

The Upper Nile Valley

EGYPT | AFRICA

Lined with a lush ribbon of date-palm groves and liberally scattered with the soaring temples of Ancient Egypt, the Upper Nile Valley between Luxor and Aswan has provided inspiration for authors, artists, and filmmakers for centuries. This winding river route's blend of languid beauty and mind-boggling history has appeared in countless novels written by both local and visiting authors.

Aswan Old Cataract Hotel

Five-star luxury and five-star literary cred. This 19th-century grand-dame hotel hosted Agatha Christie, and was amply used as a setting in *Death on the Nile*. Tea on the terrace, overlooking the Nile, is a must for fans.

sofitel.accor.com

Temples of Abu Simbel

Egypt's most dramatic temple complex is guarded by four mammoth statues of Ramses II. In *Death on the Nile*, a boulder falls from the temple cliff face, narrowly missing the heiress Linnet.

Abu Simbel, Aswan Governorate

Luxor Winter Palace Hotel

The grand chandelier and Persian carpet-clad salons of Luxor's Winter Palace immerse guests in the regal ambience of the early 20th century. Everyone who was anyone—including Agatha Christie—bedded down here.

sofitel.accor.com

SS Sudan Nile Boat

The Nile's only remaining paddle steamer, the SS *Sudan* has been restored to its original glory. Now, travelers can re-create Christie's 1933 trip, complete with all the bells and whistles.

steam-ship-sudan.com

"The Egyptian temples bore me profoundly," French novelist Gustave Flaubert wrote in 1850, after watching his Egyptian crew toil to clear the dunes and reveal Ramses II's colossal stone face at Abu Simbel. Despite the contrary diary entry, Flaubert's Nile journey was the catalyst that shook him from his writing slump. Many writers (including Youssef Ziedah and Penelope Lively) have followed in his wake.

The best known is Agatha Christie, who first visited Egypt at age 17, and returned several times during the 1930s with her archaeologist husband, Max Mallowan. Their 1933 trip on the luxury paddle steamer the SS *Sudan* directly inspired Christie's Hercule Poirot detective novel *Death on the Nile*; in the company of European aristos, the pair cruised past Egyptian monuments, just like the unlucky guests on the fictional SS *Karnak*.

Agatha Christie

Sinan Books Poetry Store

Shanghai

CHINA | ASIA

Shanghai's legendary skyline might steal the spotlight, but China's bustling megacity isn't all business. A myriad of writers have dramatized its turbulent history, making it the center of Chinese literature, both past and present.

Sheer numbers all but guarantee China's place in world literature: this ancient civilization reaches back thousands of years and the country is also home to the world's most common mother tongue. But statistics alone can't account for the accomplishments or the influence of Chinese writers, who have won Nobel Prizes and shaped thought throughout Asia.

Shanghai—international and outward-facing—has been the locus of Chinese literature since the 1920s, when prominent writers were drawn here by its relative intellectual freedom. Among them was Lu Xun, often considered the founder of modern Chinese literature, and Mao Dun, whose 1933 novel *Midnight* captured the era's glamour and tumult. That mix, so quintessentially Shanghainese, has defined many works set in the city, from Eileen Chang's romantic World War II spy novella *Lust, Caution* to Wei Hui's frenetic depiction of the 1990s party scene, *Shanghai Baby*. The city has proven equally irresistible to foreign writers, providing the setting for novels by André Malraux, Kazuo Ishiguro, and many others. Travelers, too, are sure to fall under its spell, seduced by traces of that early-20th-century drama and awed by modern celebrations of China's ancient literary heritage.

GETTING AROUND

With 18 lines connecting city districts, the Shanghai metro is the best transportation option. The city also has an extensive bus system.

READING LIST

When We Were Orphans

Kazuo Ishiguro

Set in Shanghai between the world wars, Ishiguro's novel follows a British-born detective who, haunted by his childhood, tries to solve the mystery of his missing parents.

Empire of the Sun

J. G. Ballard

Based on Ballard's own experiences, this coming-of-age novel traces a young boy's survival during the Japanese occupation of Shanghai. A film adaptation came out in 1987.

The Song of Everlasting Sorrow

Wang Anyi

Spanning four decades, Anyi's masterpiece chronicles the life of a woman in Shanghai, exploring love, loss, and the city's transformation between the 1940s and the 1980s.

Duolun Road Cultural Street

Duolun Road Cultural Street

Amid Shanghai's modernity, atmospheric Duolun Road is a vestige of the past, a pedestrianized street of handsome old homes, teahouses, and curio shops. In the 1920s and 1930s, this old-school area was home to many of China's leading progressive writers, several of whom still linger in the form of bronze statues. Down a small lane near the street's midpoint is the building, now a museum, where Lu Xun and other prominent authors founded the League of Left-Wing Writers in 1930. Counting major figures like Rou Shi and Mao Dun among its members, the group promoted socialist realism through their work and magazines; they remain essential figures in Shanghai's literary history. Nearly 100 years later, a stroll along Duolun's cobblestones (ticking off the statues as you go) is bound to inspire.

Duolun Road, Hongkou

Lu Xun Park

No figure in modern Chinese literature looms larger than Lu Xun. Born in 1881, he came to prominence in 1918 with the publication of "Diary of a Madman," the first short story written entirely in vernacular Chinese. Celebrated for his fiction, essays, academic studies, and translations, Lu Xun spent his last years in Shanghai, where he liked to take walks in Hongkou Park. Renamed Lu Xun Park in 1988, the green space mixes elements of English and Chinese gardens and is popular with elderly tai chi practitioners. Lu Xun's tomb is located at the park's center, while a memorial hall displays his belongings and sells translations of his most famous works. South of the park, fans can also visit the writer's former home, where he died in 1936.

2288 N Sichuan Road, Hongkou

Zikawei Library

This contemporary library in the Xuhui district encapsulates Shanghai's blend of Chinese and Western cultures. Its façade recalls the nearby Bibliotheca Zi-Ka-Wei, an early-20th-century depository built by Jesuit missionaries, while the interior was conceived as a series of concentric spaces, like traditional Chinese nesting boxes. Step inside and you'll find yourself in a three-story atrium, where long reading tables line up beneath a soaring, barrel-vaulted ceiling. At the far end is a 3D-printed pagoda, its white lattice-work seemingly as delicate and evanescent as a spiderweb. On the second and third floors are balconies that, through narrow columns inspired by the Bibliotheca, serve up views of Shanghai's many skyscrapers, a hedge-filled plaza, and St. Ignatius Cathedral, the latter more than a century old. Hunker down on one of the wooden bleachers for a read with a view.

158 N Caoxi Road, Xuhui; library.sh.cn

Shanghai Library East

Rising above the treetops like a wayward iceberg is the dazzling Shanghai Library East. Designed by the Danish architectural firm Schmidt Hammer Lassen and completed in 2022, the building appears as an angular white massif; look closer and you'll notice subtle marbled patterns swirling across its façade. Inside, the smooth surface gives way to textured spaces that stack, interlock, and morph as you move about, an effect meant to mimic *taihu* stones (oddly shaped rocks filled with perforations and hollows that functioned as muses for ancient scholars). Tucked into the library's dramatic spaces are site-specific works by contemporary Chinese and international artists, and numerous hard-at-work students. Turn your gaze outward and you'll be treated to views of Shanghai's skyline or the sprawling Century Park.

300 Hehuan Road, Pudong; library.sh.cn

Shanghai Book City

Where does a bookstore fit in the modern world? Shanghai Book City's (SBC) answer is twofold. First, it can't be an escape from the city around it, but must be an integral part. SBC's glittering exterior—an effect created by light shining through perforated aluminum panels—lures pedestrians to its windows, which reveal the bustling activity occurring inside. Those windows frame SBC's "Book Mountain," a vast terraced space for reading, exhibitions, and socializing. And that gets at the second part of the answer. A modern bookstore must also be comprehensive, offering things you can't find online. At SBC, that means writers' studios, wellness classrooms, cafés, galleries, and more—the idea being that anyone coming for those things might end up staying for the shop's 400,000-plus books.

465 Fuzhou Road, Huangpu

Sinan Books Poetry Store

Plenty of places have been called temples of literature. Few take the description as seriously as the Sinan Books Poetry Store. The building it occupies was built in 1932 as St. Nicholas Russian Orthodox church. It subsequently went through reincarnations as an office, canteen, and restaurant before it was resurrected as Shanghai's largest poetry bookstore in 2019. Pass beneath a carved archway to reach the soul of the building, where huge metal bookshelves ascend to a domed ceiling and a fresco of winged cherubs. Whether by the Holy Spirit or by heavenly verse, it's hard not to be moved in a place like this.

No 16 Gaolan Road, Huangpu

Sinan Books Poetry Store

Starfield Library

Seoul

SOUTH KOREA | ASIA

South Korea's capital conjures up images of K-pop and cutting-edge tech, but it also possesses a centuries-old literary pedigree—one that the design-obsessed city has a knack for putting on beautiful display.

If K-pop and K-dramas are the surging crest of Hallyu, or the Korean Wave—the pop culture phenomenon that has swept up fans around the world—the country's literature is the deep, churning water propping that wave up and carrying it to shore.

This is, after all, the world's only country with a holiday dedicated to its alphabet. It's also the birthplace of modern printing, where Buddhist monks published the world's oldest extant book created with movable metal type, a full seven decades before the ink dried on Gutenberg's Bible. Developments like these fostered a rich literary culture here—one that, centuries later, has led to the TV scripts and K-pop lyrics shaping pop culture today. But in a poetic turnabout, the success of music and film has also spurred interest in Korean literature.

The country's capital, Seoul, offers a chance to explore the history and places that have influenced Korea's famed authors. Nearly as exciting, however, are the spaces the city devotes to its books. Visitors will encounter alfresco libraries, decades-old bookstores, and architecturally stunning modern repositories. They'll also find ample opportunity to indulge in an unimprovable Korean experience: curling up on the courtyard terrace of a traditional *hanok* and sinking into a story as the sun sets.

GETTING AROUND

Seoul's metro system is comprehensive and fully integrated with the extensive bus network; rechargeable T-Money transportation cards allow passengers to transfer seamlessly between them.

READING LIST

Who Ate Up All the Shinga?

Park Wan-suh

This classic autobiographical account of life in Seoul takes place during the Japanese occupation of Korea and the Korean War.

The Vegetarian

Han Kang

Han Kang's disturbing exploration of shame and traditional gender roles is set in modern-day Seoul. Kang won the Nobel Prize in Literature in 2024.

Love in the Big City

Sang Young Park

Long-listed for the International Booker Prize in 2022, this boozy romp through Seoul's nightlife was a milestone in queer Korean literature.

GRAPHIC X DAISHIN

Comics, known as *manhwa* here, are hugely popular in Korea, making up a large part of the country's publishing industry and providing the source material for all sorts of TV shows. While a lot of *manhwa* has migrated online, print remains common, and you'll find *manhwa-bang*, shops for renting and reading comics, throughout Seoul. Most are pretty basic—not much more than bookshelves, sofas, and packs of instant ramen for sale—but some offer a more stylish experience. With contemporary furniture, atmospheric lighting, and plants, GRAPHIC X DAISHIN brings a bit of class to the *manhwa-bang* experience. Seats are reserved, and payment is by the hour. Bonus: *manhwa's* visual format means you don't even need to speak (or read) Korean to enjoy a story.

387 Wiryesunhwan-ro, Songpa-gu; graphic.fan

Itaewon Books

Itaewon Books

Paris has Shakespeare and Company *(p.112)*; Seoul has Itaewon Books. The two may not be remotely comparable in terms of fame or pedigree, but the role they play is the same. This is where expats in Korea have been coming for their literary fix since 1974. If you like your bookstores bright, airy, and latte-scented, keep moving. If you're too busy reading to worry about how things look, this is the place for you. Outside, there isn't even a sign that says "Itaewon Books," just one announcing "BOOK" in English and Korean and another above the awning reading "Foreign Book Store." Inside, books are crammed haphazardly on shelves and stacked in piles on the floor. Is there a method to this madness? Who knows. The only certain thing is that you won't find the book you came for, but you'll leave with half a dozen others instead.

208 Noksapyeong-daero, Yongsan-gu

Blue Square Book Park Lounge

Located in the trendy Hannam-dong neighborhood, Blue Square Book Park Lounge is one of Seoul's most stylish spots for a reading break. On the third floor of Blue Square, a major performing arts venue, it features hanging plants, light fixtures shaped like stacked books, and an enormous bookshelf that extends the length of a five-story atrium. Bring your own book or choose from the more than 3,000 titles curated by the literary experts here; then settle into one of the many reading areas scattered throughout the lounge. There are private nooks for deep concentration, sofas to sprawl out on, and a sunny terrace for alfresco reading. In keeping with the venue's lounge identity, you have to pay a modest entry fee, but it's valid for a full day and includes a drink at the on-site café.

294 Itaewon-ro, Yongsan-gu; bluesquare.kr

Songpa Book Museum

Songpa Book Museum

If you'd like to learn about the history of literature in Korea, this charming museum is a must-visit. Housed in a building designed to resemble the pages of a book, it explores writing from the Joseon Dynasty (1392–1910) to the present day. You can discover old writing desks and view a display devoted to the personal objects that have shaped modern authors' writing habits. After exploring the exhibits, head to the central staircase; it's lined with bookshelves and reading nooks. And, before you go, be sure to use the historic letterpress—it creates gorgeous bookmarks.

77 Songpa-daero 37-gil, Songpa-gu; songpa.go.kr

Seoul Outdoor Library

A few years ago, the Seoul Metropolitan Library (SML) was concerned about declining reading rates. Maybe the problem was phones. Maybe it was social media. Or maybe it was walls. To boost people's interest in reading, the SML decided to bring its books into the streets, and in 2022 it launched the Seoul Outdoor Library (summer weekend pop-ups in three of the city's key locations). At Seoul Plaza, the lawn is filled with colorful beanbag chairs. In Gwanghwamun Square, bookshelves stand near Seoul's main palace. And at the Cheonggyecheon Stream, lanterns are provided for nighttime reading.

Various locations; seouloutdoorlibrary.kr

Tongmungwan

Surviving as an independent bookseller is hard. Surviving as an independent bookseller through colonial occupation, civil war, and military dictatorship is even harder. Somehow, though, Tongmungwan has managed it, and today this little shop in Seoul's historic Insa-dong neighborhood stands as the city's oldest bookstore, having been open since 1934. Don't expect to find the latest potboiler or breezy beach read, though. Tongmungwan specializes in old and rare books, things like family histories, Joseon Dynasty–era ceremonial guides, and centuries-old volumes printed with woodblocks. Many are valued at more than $1,000. The tomes' old Chinese characters might be impenetrable to most travelers, but anyone who loves the physicality of books—their anti-screenness—will find something genuinely moving about being surrounded by so much history.

☞ 55-1 Insadong-gil, Jongno-gu; tongmunkwan.co.kr

Sooyeonsanbang

Seongbuk-dong has a case for being Seoul's most literary neighborhood. This peaceful area in the Bukhansan Mountain foothills was home to many important 20th-century writers, from a monk and independence activist to a president of the Society of Korean Poets. The most prominent was the novelist Lee Tae-jun, who lived in this house just off the main street from 1933 to 1946. Today, it's owned by his granddaughter, who has turned it into one of the city's loveliest teahouses. She's preserved not only the building, a traditional tile-roofed *hanok*, but also many of Lee's possessions: books rest in glass cases and a family portrait hangs on the wall. Take a seat, unwind with a cup of green plum tea, and join the lineage of Sooyeonsanbang, whose name means "a mountain home where literati gather."

☞ 8 Seongbuk-ro 26-gil, Seongbuk-gu; blog.naver.com/sooyeonsanbang1998

Cheongun Literature Library

The best libraries are more than just book repositories, they also link people, pages, and places. The first floor of Cheongun Literature Library is a typical array of shelves and desks, but head up to the second-floor reading room and you'll find yourself in a traditional *hanok* of honey-colored wood, paper windows, and handmade roof tiles. Outside, a small waterfall tumbles into a pond. Looming above the library is Mount Inwangsan—sacred to shamanists and Buddhists—and a portion of Seoul's old city walls, which have stood since 1396. You couldn't script a better setting to read a Korean classic, maybe *Memorabilia of the Three Kingdoms* or *The Story of Hong Gildong*. So pull out a cushion and get lost in the world of your book, which, in this spectacular library, is also the world around you.

☞ 40 Jahamun-ro 36-gil, Jongno-gu; lib.jongno.go.kr

Starfield Library

How many shopping malls have a library at their center? It can't be many, but that's just what you'll find in Starfield COEX Mall: a sanctuary of the written word secreted amid a shrine to commerce. You've almost certainly seen photos of Starfield Library already: the depository is a social media favorite, drawing tourists and influencers who come to film themselves riding the escalator past its two-story bookshelf or to pose, intellectually, with a carefully angled book. Dismissing Starfield as a mere stage would be unfair, though. The 30,140-sq-ft (2,800-sq-m) beauty holds more than 70,000 books, and while none of these are in English, many of its more than 600 magazine titles are. In fact, the project was so successful that Starfield opened another mall-turned-library branch in 2024, Starfield Library Suwon, and as you'd expect, it's equally spectacular.

☞ 513 Yeongdong-daero, Gangnam-gu; starfield.co.kr

Sooyeonsanbang

Labels in a secondhand bookstore in Jimbocho

Tokyo

JAPAN | ASIA

Bookstores hidden down bustling alleyways. Streetscapes pulled from the pages of beloved manga. Museums dedicated to literary greats. Cozy coffee shops frequented by contemporary authors. Meet Japan's most literary city.

It all started with *The Tale of Genji*. Written by noblewoman and poet Murasaki Shikibu, this 1,000-year-old novel (c. 1020) is said to be the world's first—meaning Japan has a literary lineage older than entire countries. Since Shikibu wrote out her tale on a folded manuscript, storytelling here has taken many forms. Manga (comic or graphic novels) surfaced way back in the 13th (some say 12th) century, though their current form largely took shape in the 1950s. Haikū were perfected by Matsuo Bashō in the 17th century, capturing life's fleeting moments in just 17 syllables. The traditional novel came to the fore under 20th-century icon Natsume Sōseki, and was later perfected by the likes of Haruki Murakami, Mieko Kawakami, and Sayaka Murata. And then came the rise of the web-novel: uber-portable, phone-friendly stories.

There's room for all these forms in Tokyo. Museums celebrate the writers of the past and tales of the future. Snazzy new spaces stock manga and contemporary fiction, while secondhand bookstores stand strong—there's even an entire "book town" (Jimbocho) devoted to them. Jazz bars welcome Murakami readers, cute coffee shops embrace fans of Toshikazu Kawaguchi, and libraries are, as always, open to all.

GETTING AROUND

For a megacity, Tokyo is surprisingly walkable. Distant districts are linked by an efficient rail network (all well-signed in English), but once you emerge onto the streets, you'll find it very pedestrian-friendly.

READING LIST

Before the Coffee Gets Cold

Toshikazu Kawaguchi

This moving story revolves around a café that offers its customers the opportunity to travel back in time, as long as they return before their coffee cools. This is the first in what has become a series.

Nana

Ai Yazawa

A popular manga series set in Tokyo that tells the story of Nana Osaki and Nana Komatsu, who meet by chance on a train and become roommates and close friends.

Kokoro

Natsume Sōseki

Meaning "heart" in Japanese, this three-part novel is a thought-provoking meditation on loneliness, guilt, and ego by one of the greatest novelists of the Meiji period.

An alley in Golden Gai, home to Open Book

Open Book

In a city of skyscrapers, Golden Gai is a breath of fresh air. Around 200 bars in low-rise buildings are squeezed into an area no larger than a couple of blocks, the alleys coming to life each night in a blaze of colorful signs, delicious scents, and overlapping songs spilling from stairwells and half-open doors. Amid all the themed bars—rockabilly, death metal, miniature plastic toys—Open Book celebrates books. Behind its wooden frontage, bookshelves run floor to ceiling, with most volumes inherited from author Komimasa Tanaka, the owner's grandfather. Despite having no sign, the bar (standing room only) always fills up quickly: arrive early, order a signature lemon sour, and either pull a book off the shelf or start chatting with your neighbor.

Alley 5, 1-1-6 Kabuki-chō, Shinjuku-ku, Golden Gai; openbook.tokyo

Kamome Books

With its cobbled streets and traditional houses, Kagurazaka is a popular setting for a lot of cozy Tokyo literature. Stroll through the neighborhood and you'll see why—its blend of traditional Japanese and European aesthetics is uniquely charming. On those days when the cobbles are gleaming with rain, make a beeline for the weathered awning that simply says "BOOK + COFFEE + GALLERY" (all the good stuff). Step inside to browse the thoughtfully curated shelves of Kamome Books, admire the gallery space or take a window seat at Weekenders Coffee All Right (the on-site café) and watch the rain fall. It's the perfect place to immerse yourself in the atmosphere of this cultural district.

123 Yarai-chō, Shinjuku-ku, Kagurazaka; kamomebooks.jp

Natsume Sōseki Memorial Museum

As Natsume Sōseki warns in his novel *Kokoro*, "You don't really become a finer person just by reading lots of books," but the consensus in Japan seems to be that reading a lot of *his* books does you some good (he remains one of the country's most widely read modern authors). Along with *Kokoro* (1914), his best-known work is *I Am a Cat* (1906), hence the images of black cats you'll find dotted throughout this museum, built on the site where he spent his final years. You'll also discover a peaceful library, a range of exhibitions and the relaxing Café Sōseki, where you can enjoy some of the writer's favorite snacks while looking out at the garden. Don't miss the re-creation of Sōseki's early-20th-century study. A low writing desk sits on a red rug, surrounded by piles of neatly stacked books and a cast-iron kettle kept warm and in reach, just as he liked it.

7 Waseda Minami-chō, Shinjuku-ku, Waseda; soseki-museum.jp

Waseda International House of Literature

The Haruki Murakami Library (as it's also known) isn't just named after the famous author; his works and interests are at its core. The library grew from the archive Murakami donated to his alma mater, and the author collaborated with architect Kengo Kuma to create the space. A café serves up great coffee and there's a replica of Murakami's study, whose mid-century touches informed the library's design. Visitors can also play a record in the audio room—perhaps The Beatles' "Norwegian Wood (This Bird Has Flown)," in honor of Murakami's famous novel.

Building 4, 1-6 Nishi-Waseda, Shinjuku-ku, Waseda

Bashō Memorial Hall

Bashō was the master of short poems, so it's fitting that the museum dedicated to him is small but perfectly formed. Sitting on the quieter eastern bank of the Sumida River, it's a peaceful spot to retreat to when you need a break from the bustle of the city and a little inspiration. Inside, a short film (with English subtitles) introduces you to the life and work of this wandering poet, while exhibitions explore his extensive travels and the hundreds of playful and poignant haikū he composed. Outside, there's a small, traditional garden and views of the river—the perfect place to write your own haikū.

1-6-3 Tokiwa, Kōtō-ku, Tokiwa

Waseda International House of Literature

Kitazawa Bookstore

Kitazawa Building

With its old-fashioned *kissaten* (Shōwa-style coffee houses) and dozens of highly specialized bookstores, Jimbocho is the ideal destination for book lovers, and the Kitazawa Building is a perfect first stop. Its focus is the atmospheric Kitazawa Bookstore, a Jimbocho mainstay since 1902. There's a pleasantly academic feel here, all dark-wood shelves and leather-bound tomes, and as the window says, it is best known for "foreign books, second-hand & rare books." The ground floor of the building, meanwhile, is home to Book House Café, which sells a great range of children's literature. Enter through the nondescript door at the back, instead, and you'll find yourself in the semi-hidden Bar Lilliput, a cozy spot stocked with picture books and jazz records.

2-5 Kanda-Jimbocho, Chiyoda-ku, Jimbocho; kitazawa.co.jp & bookhousecafe.jp

Museum of Modern Japanese Literature

Tomigaya feels like the cool older cousin of neighboring Shibuya, the high-energy center of Tokyo's youth culture. It's the kind of place where you while away afternoons in specialized coffee shops, independent boutiques and galleries. It's also home to several top museums, including the elegant edifice of the Museum of Modern Japanese Literature. Housing important pieces of the country's literary history—including handwritten letters and manuscripts by authors like Ryūnosuke Akutagawa and Nobel Prize–winner Yasunari Kawabata—as well as temporary exhibitions, it's a popular spot for bookish types (though it's worth noting that English translations are rather lacking). Once you've explored, head to the on-site café, where you can borrow a book to read.

4-3-55 Komaba, Meguro-ku, Tomigaya; bungakukan.or.jp

Daikanyama T-Site

Tsutaya is one of Japan's biggest bookstore chains, with shops across the country. Tokyo has several excellent branches, but if you only have time to visit one, make it Daikanyama T-Site. Designed as a "Library in the Woods," the beloved bookstore is spread across three modern, interconnected buildings set in leafy surroundings in a chic neighborhood. There are book concierges on hand to help you find just the right read—there are always some foreign-language titles here—but you're also welcome to lose yourself among the many, many shelves. It's a relaxing place to wander, with ambient lighting and comfy furniture dotted around. But once you've found the perfect volume, don't rush off just yet. Instead, cozy up with a drink in the literary-themed Anjin Lounge, where bookworms hunker down and friends flip through magazines. Or, if you're inspired to write something of your own, join freelance creatives in the quiet surroundings of the Share Lounge coworking space—you can pay for a pass that gives you unlimited food and drinks here.

17-5 Sarugaku-chō, Shibuya-ku, Daikanyama; store.tsite.jp

BOOK AT BEDTIME

Manga Art Hotel

On the edge of Jimbocho this 35-bed capsule hotel *(mangaarthotel.com)* is dedicated to comic books, with more than 5,000 titles. Rather than sleep, it's a place dedicated to capturing that feeling of staying up all night, telling yourself, "Just one more chapter ...."

Morioka Shōten

Do you get decision paralysis? Have you sworn off book hauls to avoid *tsundoku* (piles of unread books)? Then Morioka Shōten is the place for you. More gallery than bookshop, this tiny space on the fringes of glitzy Ginza describes itself as "a single room with a single book." Every week, Morioka Shōten showcases a different work, and the space is decorated to reflect it. You might find a hefty photo book, with images displayed on the walls; a memoir, with the author on hand for discussion; or maybe even just the delicate curls of smoke from incense, with the instruction to "read" the scent. It's certainly not your typical bookstore experience, but it encapsulates the creativity, risk-taking and commitment to excellence that makes Tokyo the strange, wonderful, unforgettable city that it is.

1-28-15 Chūō-ku, Ginza; moriokabook.theshop.jp

Tama Cemetery

If Paris has Père Lachaise *(p.117)* and London has Highgate, then Tokyo has Tama. In the city's sleepy western reaches, this cemetery is a huge and beautiful green space. Between the reaching trunks of pine trees and the springtime froth of cherry blossoms are the resting places of several significant historical figures, from politicians to ballerinas, artists to athletes. But that's not all. The graves of some of the country's brightest literary lights are also in these leafy grounds, including Yosano Akiko, pioneering feminist poet and social reformer; Yukio Mishima, known as much for his extreme right-wing views as his poetic, existential tales; Edogawa Ranpo, the master of mysteries whose pen name is a rendering of "Edgar Allan Poe"; and Nakamura Fusetsu, who illustrated *I Am a Cat*.

4-628 Tama-chō, Fuchū-shi, Tama; tokyo-park.or.jp/reien/tama

Jimbocho Book Town

With well over 100 bookstores, Jimbocho's pedigree as Tokyo's "book town" is uncontested. During Japan's rapid modernization in the late 19th century, several universities established campuses in this area—and where there are scholars, booksellers naturally follow.

DISTANCE
1.5 miles (2 km)

WALKING TIME
Allow an hour

NEAREST TRANSIT
Jimbocho has its own subway station (on the Hanzōmon, Mita, and Shinjuku lines)

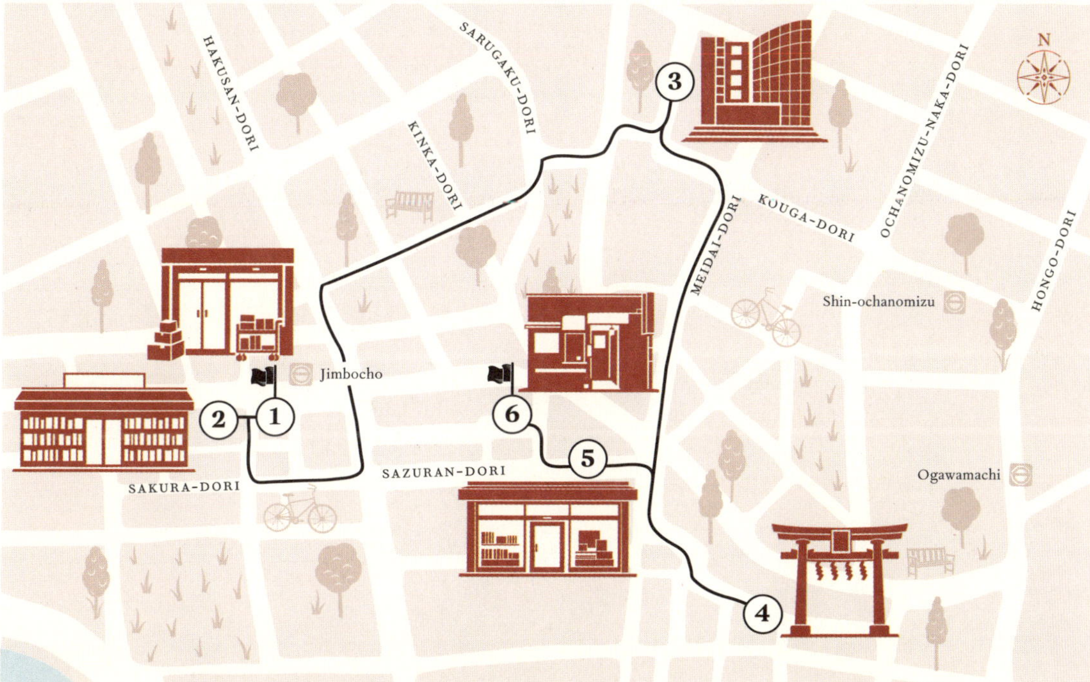

1. Takayama Honten

Founded in 1875, this spot has a strong claim to be Jimbocho's oldest bookstore. Its packed shelves are mostly dedicated to works on Japan's traditional performing arts *(Yasukuni-dori)*.

2. Yaguchi Shoten

An icon on an equally iconic street, this quaint bookstore is famed for its outdoor shelves packed with secondhand books. The road itself, Yasukuni-dori, marks the heart of Jimbocho *(2 Chome 5–1)*.

3. Meiji University Museum

Meiji University is one of the prestigious institutions of learning founded here in the late 1800s, and its museum is a great place to explore the district's academic side *(1–1 Kanda Surugadai)*.

4. Gotō Inari-jinja

This small, peaceful shrine is known for its frequently changing *goshu-in* (shrine stamps with elegant calligraphy) and beautiful *goshuin-chō* (stamp books) *(3 Chome 9–1)*.

5. Bohemian's Guild

Like many Jimbocho bookstores, Bohemian's Guild is specialized. The focus here is on arts and culture, with books downstairs and art and calligraphy upstairs *(Kanda Suzuran-dori)*.

6. Ladrio

Days at the Morisaki Bookshop fans will love Ladrio, a likely inspiration for the book's Saveur café. The real thing has the same soothing ambience as in Satoshi Yagisawa's book *(1 Chome 3–3)*.

Street scene in Bangkok

Bangkok

THAILAND | ASIA

Bangkok glistens in our imagination, a scorching, sunlit city of golden temples and shimmering skyscrapers. The reality is much cooler: a hip metropolis where elegant libraries, chic bookstores, and literary cafés await.

The world's fascination with Bangkok echoes throughout centuries of literature. Famous international writers have come and gone, including Polish-British novelist Joseph Conrad, who sailed to Siam (as Thailand was then known) and made the capital a figure in a handful of his books. Over a century later, writer and director Alex Garland chose Bangkok's traveler hub, Khao San Road, as the starting point of a backpacker's dream-turned-nightmare in his novel *The Beach*.

The Beach immortalized Bangkok as backpacker heaven, but Thailand's young capital (founded in 1782) is so much more than cheap drinks and late-night bars. Just look at the city's literary scene. Bangkok is a UNESCO World Book Capital, thanks to the city's numerous reading campaigns and the plethora of bookish spaces encouraging Bangkokians to pick up a paperback. There are grand libraries, low-key bookstores, and cute literary cafés aplenty; they're perfect places to escape the hubbub of the city, and to get to know Bangkok from a local perspective. Swap Conrad for Thai writers Pitchaya Sudbanthad or Rattawut Lapcharoensap and you'll learn all about the sticky rainy season, the mouth-watering cuisine, and the families that inhabit this great city.

GETTING AROUND

Bangkokians stick to the air-conditioned BTS trains or "motorcy" taxis that swerve through traffic like figure skaters; you can flag the latter down on an app called Grab. Both options are cheap and scenic.

READING LIST

Four Reigns

Kukrit Pramoj

This historical novel follows Phloi, a woman born into a minor noble family. She lives through the reigns of four Thai kings from the end of the 1880s to the mid-1940s.

Sightseeing

Rattawut Lapcharoensap

A vibrant collection of short stories set in contemporary Thailand, *Sightseeing* explores themes of familial ties, young love, and generational conflict.

Bangkok Wakes to Rain

Pitchaya Sudbanthad

This sweeping, multigenerational story follows numerous characters through numerous decades in their lives. It's highly original storytelling and a searing portrait of the city.

Bangkok City Library

Locals love the Bangkok City Library. Why? First of all, because of its design. This bookish haunt is housed in a renovated branch of the Bank of Thailand. It's a gorgeous, three-story, Art Deco building with lofty ceilings and elegant finishes, but there are modern features, too: huge windows line spacious rooms, where there's seemingly endless desk space. Secondly, the library is right in the center of Bangkok (between the royal palace and the raucous Khao San Road), making it a perfect break from the buzz. Thirdly, and perhaps most importantly in a city famed for its sweat-inducing weather, it's very well air-conditioned. Come for an hour to grab coffee from the bar, cool down, and flick through the English-language magazines.

39 Ratchadamnoen Klang Road, Royal City; +66 2 282 0680

Bangkok City Library

Book Lovers Books

In a time before Kindles, backpackers dreamed of finding cheap bookstores like this. A mirage from the past, Book Lovers Books is a laid-back little spot with a makeshift yellow sign hanging outside that simply says "BOOKS." Inside, pre-loved titles are piled up on plain shelves, and there's not much in the way of decor. But don't let the lack of frills put you off; this place has a big heart. It's run by a devoted family, who kept the shop open during the COVID-19 pandemic and even offered to personally drop off books to customers who called up in need of some literary medicine. You'll find the shop parallel to Khao San Road, and as you'd expect, it features a great English-language section for backpackers—perfect for picking up a beach read for your travels.

59 Ram Buttri Alley, Royal City

Passport Bookshop

This cutesy independent bookstore and café is a delight through and through. The owners have taken twee design and run with it: think old TV stands as display tables, chintzy crockery, and floral tablecloths your grandma would likely adore. There are even sweet handwritten recommendations dotting the meticulously curated shelves. It's so homey and welcoming that staying for hours is entirely plausible—particularly if you settle down in the café for a delicious scone or two (best served with a pot of tea). This local gem has been selling books for some 20 years, offering both Thai- and English-language titles. It's also one of the best spots in central Bangkok to pick up unique, arty postcards, which line the teal-colored shopfront as you enter.

28 Soi Samran Rat, Royal City

World at the Corner

World at the Corner

World at the Corner's name makes sense as soon as you step through its doors. The shelves are stocked full of titles about other countries and cultures, encompassing everything from art to fashion to food. Whatever you pick up will whisk you away, as will the shop's evocative music, unique international ornaments, and fragrant incense smoke twirling toward the ceiling. The shop is a labor of love run by local photographers Nat and Sivika Prakobsantisuk, and it's a wonderful pit stop for anyone in need of some travel inspiration.

1 Mahannop 1 Alley, Royal City; readthecloud.co/world-at-the-corner-bookshop

Burapasarn

Burapasarn is the customer-facing bookstore of the long-established publishing house of the same name. For readers of the local language, there's a host of gorgeous books here—think astrology, arts, psychology, and science. For those not fluent in Thai, it's still a lovely place to browse. Better yet, the bookshop's café, Burapa Coffee, is a great spot to sit and read your own book, or do some writing; it's friendly yet tranquil, quite the opposite to the din from the busy neighborhood outside. The iced brews and baked treats are pretty good, too.

120 Charoen Krung Road, Royal City; burapasarnbook.com

Neilson Hays Library

Founded back in 1869, the Neilson Hays Library remains faithful to its original ethos: an English-language lending library that serves the local community with bookish events for all ages. Its current incarnation is housed in a sumptuous Neo-Classical building from the 1920s (which, in ever-changing Bangkok, is pretty old), with white Ionic columns and glossy teak-wood paneling. It's just 100 THB (£2.50) to enter for the day, allowing tourists to trawl through the vast collection of fiction, nonfiction, and kids' books (though you can't take any home). If you're staying in town for longer, consider an annual membership.

195 Surawong Road, Bang Rak; neilsonhayslibrary.org

BOOK AT BEDTIME

The Mandarin Oriental

The riverside Mandarin Oriental *(mandarinoriental.com)* is the most prestigious stay in Bangkok. Writers like Joseph Conrad and Graham Greene once slept here, and they're memorialized in the hotel's Author's Lounge, which serves afternoon tea.

Neilson Hays Library

Balzac

Around the corner from Bangkok's French Embassy, Swiss proprietor Zak opened the cultural center Balzac as an homage to all things Francophone. He expected largely French-speaking people to drop by, but Thai locals came too, drawn by Balzac's grass-green façade and bright, light-flooded café-bookstore. And kudos to Zak, you'd be forgiven for thinking you're in Paris here: the elegant walls are lined with quintessentially French posters, photos, and artwork, while *chansons françaises* play on the stereo and the most incredible crêpes are served. Perhaps unsurprisingly, Balzac is always packed with regulars, who catch up with friends over a croque monsieur before browsing the three floors of books.

Soi Charoen Krung 43 Charoen Krung 357, Bang Rak; balzacbangkok.com

Balzac

A Book with No Name

Obsessed with the classics? So is this part-café, part-bookstore. Portraits of literary luminaries like Ernest Hemingway *(p.112)*, George Orwell, and Virgina Woolf *(p.87)* decorate the walls, and drinks on the menu are named after beloved authors—the F. Scott Fitzgerald/Gatsby Coffee is a delicious brew featuring an espresso shot and tonic water, for example. This quirky, independent outfit is staffed by a duo of bibliophiles, but they're not just obsessed with books. Five cute cats and a friendly little dog called Abby roam the shop and are more than happy to sit with visitors. The plethora of greenery—large leafy plants to provide shade around the entrance and smaller pots of succulents inside—also add to the vibes, making this a deliciously relaxing place to pull up a chair. The proprietors only ask that you order a beverage or sweet treat while you linger.

721, 723 Samsen 17 Alley, Dusit

Dasa Book Cafe

Another great secondhand bookseller, which actually proclaims itself the best in the city (points for swagger) is Dasa in trendy Sukhumvit. And if you like your used bookstores packed full, yet orderly, you might agree. Dasa's huge stock of more than 18,000 books is piled high and always fun to browse, but if you have authors or subjects in mind, make life easier and use the online database. As an added bonus, staff make a mean Thai Tea, iced or piping hot (Thai people usually drink it iced, given the climate).

714/4 Sukhumvit Road, Sukhumvit; dasabookcafe.com

State Library of Victoria

Melbourne

AUSTRALIA | OCEANIA

Other cities may wear their literary history firmly on their sleeve, but Melbourne's love for books appears cool and casual. Literary folk here hang out in stunning libraries, sure, but they also show up to quirky zine events and linger late in grungy bookstores.

Often thought of as Australia's capital of culture (sorry, Sydney), Melbourne earned its full literary credentials when it became the world's second ever UNESCO City of Literature in 2008. The city—whose traditional Indigenous name is Naarm—received this accolade for its vibrant mix of local writers, indie publishing houses, outstanding libraries, and buzzing bookstores.

Cut through by the Yarra River, the Victorian capital has always managed to stay edgy: it saw the publication of the early true-crime bestseller *The Mystery of a Hansom Cab* back in 1886, and the emergence of Australia's own literary genre, grunge lit. The latter reached its peak in the 1990s, with the unapologetically gritty works of local writers like Helen Garner and Christos Tsiolkas; their raw, experimental spirit lives on today—particularly in the city's thriving indie zine scene.

Melburnians will be sure to tell you that they've got their share of bookstores and libraries, but literature is also a social thing here. There are spoken-word slams galore and a whole host of literary festivals that bring readers, writers, and culture-seekers together. And it goes without saying that the city's café culture is a huge part of that—who could resist a book chat over a flat white or a "magic" (the city's unofficial coffee)?

GETTING AROUND

Melbourne's Central Business District is easy to explore on foot—or you can hop on the city's free central circular tram. Other neighborhoods are well served by other (not free) tram lines.

READING LIST

The Mystery of a Hansom Cab

Fergus Hume

Beginning with the discovery of a body, this detective mystery unravels through Melbourne's underbelly, revealing long-kept secrets and hidden identities.

Monkey Grip

Helen Garner

Depicting the bohemian life of a single mother in 1970s Melbourne, this groundbreaking feminist text interrogates addiction, relationships, and motherhood.

Loaded

Christos Tsiolkas

Taking place over 24 hours, this novel follows Ari, a young, gay Greek-Australian in a drug-fueled rejection of his family and the racist society in which he has been raised.

State Library of Victoria

Australia's oldest library might look a little dated from the outside (with its hulking columns and Classical portico), but step inside and you'll realize that it's still a buzzing space. Kids leaf through picture books in the dedicated children's area, students hang out in the social spaces, and literary folk flock to the Wheeler Centre (which hosts talks and readings). Venture deeper into the building and you might spot the bizarre suit of armor once owned by Victorian sharpshooting outlaw Ned Kelly, or a copy of his infamous *Jerilderie Letter*. But the real highlight is La Trobe Reading Room, a soaring, domed room filled with oak furniture and green reading lamps. You might imagine it's all quiet here, but true to the library's laid-back ethos, there's a steady murmur of voices and the odd "wow" from eager visitors.

☞ 328 Swanston Street, CBD; slv.vic.gov.au

The Paperback Bookshop

narrm ngarrgu Library

The name of this library (which is pronounced "nahm nar-GUW," in case you ever need to ask a Melburnian for directions) comes from the local Wurundjeri Woi-wurrung language and means "Melbourne knowledge." This 2023 addition to the city's network of libraries was designed with Australia's Indigenous cultures in mind, with First Nations stories and patterns woven into the architecture and design of the building; its carpet, for instance, honors the tribal lands of the Kulin Nation (the area's traditional custodians). There's a welcoming community feel here: you'll no doubt be seeing stitchers at work in the creator spaces, podcasters yammering away in the studios, and children discovering their local history through play. After all, whoever said libraries needed to be stuffy?

☞ 141 Therry Street, CBD; melbourne.vic.gov.au/narrm-ngarrgu-library-and-family-services

The Paperback Bookshop

There's something romantic and oh-so-literary about a little bit of dilapidation done right, and that's just what you get with the Paperback Bookshop. Found at the quiet end of Melbourne's Central Business District, this old-school spot comes complete with crumbling paint, posters glued to the walls, and books piled high in the windows. The shop started life back in the swinging sixties as an import spot for books from overseas that were otherwise banned under Australia's strict censorship rules. Fortunately for edgier Melburnian readers, the rules aren't so strict any more, but this spot on Bourke Street stays true to that clandestine vibe with its tightly packed shelves, late opening hours, and engaging Salon Series events where readers mingle with local authors.

☞ 60 Bourke Street, CBD; paperbackbooks.com.au

Melbourne Athenaeum Library

Melbourne Athenaeum Library

Remember when subscription libraries were a thing? Not many people do, but there's one still thriving on Collins Street—the Melbourne Athenaeum, which has been going strong for almost two centuries now. Back in the day, an entire family could access the collections for just £1 per year; these days, monthly membership fees cost less than the price of a flat white, and come with plenty of quiet, community vibes, plus free tea and coffee. Not a member? Don't worry; you'll still be welcomed with open arms at bookish talks and candlelit concerts (book ahead).

☞ 188 Collins Street, CBD; melbourneathenaeum.org.au/library

Hares & Hyenas

Hares & Hyenas is Melbourne's go-to spot for LGBTQ+ literature, a place that is just as much about building community as it is about building your book collection (though of course they're great for that, too). Legendary local author Christos Tsiolkas is known to hold regular talks here, and he even launched *Loaded*—one of the foundational texts of queer Melburnian lit—back in 1995 at the old Hares & Hyenas shop in Brunswick. The shop has moved location a fair bit since then, but has now found a home in the Victorian Pride Centre out in the seaside neighborhood of St. Kilda.

☞ 79-81 Fitzroy Street, St. Kilda; hares-hyenas.com.au

Readings Carlton

Readings Carlton

If you've been in town for a while, you might think you're seeing double with the number of Readings shops there are. But fear not, this isn't a big conglomerate: it's Melbourne's best-loved indie book chain. The venue on Lygon Street is the crown jewel (and flagship shop) in the Readings family, nestled away among the cafés and gelato spots of the Carlton neighborhood (also known as Little Italy). The team here are big on Aussie lit (and rightfully so), making it a great spot to sink your teeth into a novel by Alexis Wright or Gerald Murnane, two of Australia's greatest living authors. Admittedly, the shop's endless shelves of Antipodean authors may feel a little daunting to the uninitiated; happily, the staff are always on hand to dish out their best recs.

☞ 309 Lygon Street, Carlton; readings.com.au

Bunjil Place Library

Bunjil Place—a huge arts center out in the sleepy suburb of Narre Warren—takes its name from one of the most important First Nations stories: the tale of Bunjil the creator deity. According to the local Boon Wurrung and Wurundjeri peoples, Bunjil, who takes the form of a wedge-tailed eagle, brought the area's landscapes, animals, and people into being during the Dreamtime, and protected the land. The design of the library pays tribute to this story, with the curves of the roof evoking the spread of an eagle's wings (the impressive atrium offers a great view of the arched wooden underside). Inside the building, there's a well-stocked library—the perfect place to learn more about the area and its culture—and a charming reading garden and café, where locals meet to share ideas. Topping it off is an array of community-focused events, including regularly changing exhibitions, performances, and film screenings.

☞ 2 Patrick North East Drive, Narre Warren; bunjilplace.com.au

LITERARY FESTIVAL

Blak & Bright

This biannual festival (dates vary) brings Aboriginal and Torres Strait Islander writing to even greater audiences in Melbourne/Naarm. First Nations writing of all genres is championed, whether it's poetry, novels, theater, or spoken word.

Atrium at Bunjil Place

Pegasus Books

Wellington

NEW ZEALAND | OCEANIA

Think of Wellington and it's probably coffee, craft beer, and windy weather that first spring to mind. But New Zealand's pint-size capital is also a hub of the country's literary scene, with indie bookstores and community-focused libraries aplenty.

New Zealand's great writers hail from across the country, requiring a road trip (arguably the best way to explore the North and South Islands in any case) to visit the locations that inspired them. Keri Hulme (whose *The Bone People* won the Booker Prize in 1985) spent most of her time in the coastal settlement Ōkārito; Witi Ihimaera (of *The Whale Rider* fame) was raised near the city of Gisborne; and Janet Frame (a quietly groundbreaking poet and novelist) is associated with Dunedin, a UNESCO City of Literature. But for the greatest concentration of literary sites, Wellington is your best bet.

New Zealand's compact capital isn't short on natural beauty (picture a harborside city between folded green peaks), and its inspiring good looks have long made it a gathering place for artists and writers. As you explore, you might hear locals exclaiming, "You can't beat Wellington on a good day"; while they're often giving a tongue-in-cheek nod to the infamously blustery weather here, for literature lovers the saying rings true year-round thanks to Wellington's surplus of bookish sights. The city has a walking trail dedicated to local writers; a museum honoring Katherine Mansfield, one of the city's literary greats; and plenty of well-loved independent bookstores.

GETTING AROUND

Walking and cycling are great options, with the compact center just 1.2 miles (2 km) wide and crossed with cycle lanes. Buses, trains, and ferries also operate, the latter running to the South Island.

READING LIST

The Garden Party

Katherine Mansfield

Mansfield's most famous short story, "The Garden Party," examines social classes through the eyes of its young protagonist. The party setting was based on Mansfield's former family home in Wellington.

Speed of Light

Joy Cowley

Cowley's acclaimed YA novel follows Jeff, a young man from a troubled family who retreats into mathematics, until a mysterious visitor challenges his understanding of the world around him.

Unspeakable Secrets of the Aro Valley

Danyl McLauchlan

A hapless writer named Danyl gets caught up in a bizarre series of events in Wellington's underbelly.

Pegasus Books

Pegasus Books

This cozy secondhand bookstore takes its name from Pegasus, the legendary winged horse in Greek mythology who stamped his foot and created the Hippocrene, a spring that provided poetic inspiration. While you won't find any water here (it doesn't exactly mix well with paper), there's plenty of inspiration. Poetry, philosophy, mythology, and the classics are, given the shop's moniker, front and center, but by no means the only genres here; browse the packed shelves and you'll find travel, crafts, gardening, LGBTQ+ titles, and much, much more. In fact, there are so many tomes that they spill out of the warren-like rooms and onto the street, piled high in wicker baskets and on wooden carts. If it all gets a little overwhelming, the friendly, well-read staff will point you in the right direction.

☞ Cuba Mall, Left Bank, Te Aro; pegasusbooksnz.com

Te Matapihi ki te Ao Nui / Wellington Central Library

This beloved library's Māori name translates to "a window to the wider world"—and that's just what it offers. Found in the heart of Wellington and reopened in 2026 following extensive earthquake proofing, it's packed with around 370,000 mind-opening books, ranging from children's classics to best-selling novels, Māori literature to New Zealand reference books. The revamped space was designed to serve the wider community: alongside quiet reading spots and spacious areas for author talks and lectures, there are play zones for kids, recording studios to capture oral histories, and workshops for local makers. Throughout the building too are artworks honoring New Zealand's natural world.

☞ 65 Victoria Street, CBD; tematapihi.govt.nz

Unity Books

A tiny, windowless space measuring 4 ft (1.2 m) wide at its narrowest point: that was where Unity books, now a Wellington institution, first started life. It was set up in 1967 by Alan Preston, a professional sportsman who later became a philosopher. Alan stocked his shop with books on history, politics, the classics, and philosophy, gradually branching out into international literature (a rarity in the country at that time) and works by New Zealand authors and publishers. Today, the shelves in this now-spacious shop (found down the street from the original shop) are packed with every genre under the sun, and watched over by enthusiastic staff who are always ready with a recommendation; don't be surprised if they attempt to entice you to one of many bookish events: think readings, book launches, author signings, and seminars.

☞ 57 Willis Street, Wellington Central; unitybooks.co.nz

Wellington Writers Walk

Stretching around the edge of the city's harbor is a collection of 23 typographical sculptures, commissioned by the New Zealand Society of Authors. Made from either concrete or wood, they celebrate the words of renowned Kiwi writers who have links to Wellington, with quotes from the likes of novelist Elizabeth Knox, poet Bill Manhire, Māori author Patricia Grace, and, needless to say, short story writer Katherine Mansfield. Pick up a trail map from a local library or information center and get exploring: the sculptures can be found on boardwalks, on the sides of piers, and even submerged under the harbor.

Wellington Waterfront; wellingtonwriterswalk.co.nz

Katherine Mansfield House & Garden

Born and bred in Wellington, Katherine Mansfield is famed for her Modernist short stories, several of which, such as "Prelude," feature her childhood home. Built in 1888, the year of her birth, this stately house is now a museum dedicated to Mansfield's life, including her move to Europe at age 19 and untimely death of tuberculosis at 34. The interior, filled with late 19th- and early 20th-century furniture, has been restored to resemble its appearance in Mansfield's day, and dotted here and there are old sepia photographs and excerpts from her writing.

25 Tinakori Road, Thorndon; katherinemansfield.com

Katherine Mansfield House & Garden

More Bookish Places

If this book contained all the literary places in the world, it'd be a never-ending story … but here are more of our favorites.

Philadelphia

PENNSYLVANIA, US | NORTH AMERICA

Bookish Philly has it all. There are writers' homes, including Edgar Allan Poe's and Walt Whitman's; historic bookstores, such as family-run Hakim's; and a number of great libraries—check out the elegant Parkway Central and the Rosenbach Museum and Library.

Portland

OREGON, US | NORTH AMERICA

Every November, Portland Book Festival entices readers with promises of author talks, writing workshops, and a bustling book fair. More books can be found in shops like the legendary Powell's and Black-owned Third Eye Books.

Los Angeles

CALIFORNIA, US | NORTH AMERICA

California's sunlit city might be more famous for its film credentials, but that doesn't mean you should overlook its literary scene. There are plenty of great bookstores here, including Vroman's, Reparations Club, and a Barnes & Noble that occupies an old theater.

Quebec

CANADA | NORTH AMERICA

French-speaking Quebec isn't short of beautiful book repositories. Two highlights include the Morrin Centre, a fairytale old-world library, and the Maison de la littérature, a serene, vaulted space in a former Methodist church.

Toronto

CANADA | NORTH AMERICA

Canada's longest-running festival of literature occurs in Toronto, and the city is home to numerous top bookstores, but its libraries take the cake. Don't miss the eye-catching Toronto Reference Library and the Thomas Fisher Rare Book Library.

Cartagena

COLOMBIA | SOUTH AMERICA

Gabriel García Márquez once called Cartagena home, and this Colombian city is home to a number of sites dedicated to the beloved author. It also hosts the annual Hay Festival Cartagena de Indias, an international edition of the Wales-born festival *(p.92)*.

Amsterdam

NETHERLANDS | EUROPE

Anne Frank wrote her famous diary in Amsterdam while in hiding; today, her life can be explored at the poignant Anne Frank House. Elsewhere, travelers can admire the collections at the stunning Cuypers Library or browse the Oudemanhuispoort book market.

Barcelona

SPAIN | EUROPE

Hosting over 100 publishing houses, Barcelona is a bookish hot spot. Writers once flocked to historic cafés like Els Quatre Gats and Café de l'Òpera to discuss ideas; today's literati hunker down in libraries such as Ateneu Barcelonés or bookstores like Laie.

Porto

PORTUGAL | EUROPE

Porto has some truly great bookstores: old-world Moreira da Costa, bohemian Café Candelabro, and fairy tale Livraria Lello. The latter's magical vibes provided inspiration for the *Harry Potter* series, with parts of the first book written at nearby Café Majestic.

Venice

ITALY | EUROPE

Venice has long been a hangout spot for writers: Lord Byron frequented Caffè Florian and Marcel Proust loved the Grand Café Quadri. Other literary sights include the opulent Biblioteca Marciana and lots of cute bookstores (Libreria Acqua Alta oozes charm).

Rome

ITALY | EUROPE

Whether it's the Keats-Shelley House, dedicated to two of England's famed Romantic poets, or the Casa di Goethe, honoring the prolific German author, Rome bears the mark of many iconic writers. Added to this are gorgeous libraries, including Biblioteca Angelica.

Budapest

HUNGARY | EUROPE

Literary travelers should add Budapest to their bucket list for one sight alone: the Metropolitan Ervin Szabó, a magical library with spiral staircases and chandeliers. The city is also home to several museums dedicated to local writers, including the Ady Endre Emlékmúzeum.

Marrakesh

MOROCCO | AFRICA

With two literature festivals to its name, Marrakesh is a hub for book lovers. The city's streets are sprinkled with literary attractions, including the relaxed Cafe du Livre (a café-bookstore) and the arty Yves Saint Laurent Museum Library.

Alexandria

EGYPT | AFRICA

This historic city has long been a place of literature. While there is no trace of the ancient Great Library of Alexandria, the ruins of the Serapeum, its sister library, can be visited, as can the modern Bibliotheca Alexandrina, containing around 8 million books.

Cape Town

SOUTH AFRICA | AFRICA

Home of acclaimed writers such as novelist J. M. Coetzee, Cape Town has plenty to lure book lovers, including the annual Open Book Festival and the Centre for the Book, with its grand domed reading room. There are some excellent bookstores, too.

Durban

SOUTH AFRICA | AFRICA

Africa's first UNESCO City of Literature, Durban celebrates the written word with excellent bookstores like Ike's Books, top festivals such as Poetry Africa and Time of the Writer, and historic writers trails (check out those on Grey Street and in Cato Manor).

Dubai

UAE | MIDDLE EAST

Glittering Dubai offers plenty for book lovers, thanks to its superb bookshops (among them Kutubna and Magrudy's) and collection of free beachside libraries. The space-aged Mohammed bin Rashid Library is another great repository, if you're in need of shade.

Mumbai

INDIA | ASIA

Libraries are the lifeblood of literary Mumbai. They range from the 19th-century David Sassoon Library, decorated with tiled floors and chandeliers, to the Forest of Knowledge, whose arched wooden beams represent the branches of trees.

Delhi

INDIA | ASIA

Delhi has inspired countless writers, from novelist Arundhati Roy to poet Mirza Ghalib (fans of the latter can visit his house, Ghalib ki Haveli). Meanwhile, new reads lie in wait at popular spots like Kunzum, a bookstore-café, and Daryaganj Sunday Book Market.

Kolkata

INDIA | ASIA

Cultural Kolkata is famed for its reader-focused book fair and its collection of bookstores—from modern STORY, with its mirrored ceiling, to longstanding Dasgupta and Co., set up in 1886. Another highlight is College Street, home to a secondhand book market.

Singapore

SINGAPORE | ASIA

Stylish Singapore is filled with beautiful libraries: there's the light-filled Rotunda Gallery, the sumptuous Cook & Tras Social Library and the peaceful Library@Orchard. Stop by the Writers Bar at the Raffles Hotel, too—it hosted Joseph Conrad and Rudyard Kipling.

Jakarta

INDONESIA | ASIA

Books and coffee go hand in hand in Jakarta, thanks to its slew of literary cafés, like homey Taksu Book Cafe, lively Makan di Tebet, and cozy Coffee Book. Cool libraries also dot the city, among them the National Library of Indonesia (the world's tallest library).

Sydney

AUSTRALIA | OCEANIA

Buzzing Sydney is home to Australia's oldest library, the State Library of NSW, known for its gorgeous Tudor-style Shakespeare Room. There's also bookstores aplenty, including the sprawling Dymocks and community-focused Better Read Than Dead.

Dunedin

NEW ZEALAND | OCEANIA

This charming university town is packed with bookstores, among them the cozy University Book Shop. In the center, a statue of poet Robert Burns watches over the Writers' Walk, a series of brass plaques honoring authors with connections to the city.

Index

Featured cities have **bold** page numbers.

A

Abbey Bookshop, The, Paris 113
A Book with No Name, Bangkok 203
A Brasileira, Lisbon 124, 126
Ahmet Hamdi Tanpınar Edebiyat Müze Kütüphanesi, Istanbul 170
Akmar Passage, Istanbul 173
Al-Azbakiyya Book Market, Cairo 176
Albertine, New York City 16
Alcott, Louisa May 20, 25
Alexandria 216
Altstadt Vienna 137
American Writers Museum, Chicago 28
Amsterdam 215
Anne of Green Gables Museum, Prince Edward Island 57
Another Country, Berlin 142
Antiquariat an der Nikolaikirche, Leipzig 148
Aracataca 66, 68–9
Argosy, New York City 15
Armchair Books, Edinburgh 103
Assistens Churchyard, Copenhagen 157
Aswan Old Cataract Hotel 179
Atatürk Cultural Centre Library, Istanbul 172, 173
Athenaeum, Boston 20
Athenaeum Library, Melbourne 207
AUC Bookstore, Cairo 176
Auerbachs Keller, Leipzig 149
Austen, Jane 95, 96, 97
Avonlea Village, Prince Edward Island 57

B

Balzac, Bangkok 203
Balzac, Honoré de 117, 203
Bangkok **198–203**
Barcelona 215
Barnes & Noble, Chicago 29
Barnes & Noble, Washington, D.C. 32
Barrio de las Letras, Madrid 120
Bashō Memorial Hall, Tokyo 193
Bath **94–7**
Beacon Hill Books & Café, Boston 21
Berlin **140–45**
Biblioteca de México, Mexico City 60
Biblioteca Luis Ángel Arango, Bogotá 66
Biblioteca Marucelliana, Florence 132
Biblioteca Nacional de España, Madrid 121
Biblioteca Nacional de Maestros, Buenos Aires 77
Biblioteca Nacional Mariano Moreno, Buenos Aires 78, 79
Biblioteca Vasconcelos, Mexico City 58, 60
Biblioteca Virgilio Barco, Bogotá 64, 66
Bibliothèque Mazarine, Paris 112
Bibliothèque nationale de France, Paris 114, 115
BK Historic House and Gardens, New Orleans 38
Black Bird Bookstore, San Francisco 48
Black Diamond, The, Copenhagen 154, 156
Blackwell's, Oxford 91
Blixen, Karen 155, 157
Bloomsbury Group, London 87
Blue moon Tavern, Seattle 42
Blue Square Book Park Lounge, Seoul 186
Bodleian, The, Oxford 90
Bogotá **64–7**
Book City, Shanghai 183
Book Hotel Leipzig 149
Book Lovers Books, Bangkok 200
Books & Company, Copenhagen 158
Books Upstairs, Dublin 108
Boston **18–23**
Bouquinistes, Paris 113
Brattle Book Shop, Boston 18, 20
British Institute of Florence, The 131
British Library, London 84, 85
Brontë Country 98–9
Brontë sisters 13, 98–9
Budapest 215
Buenos Aires **74–9**
Bunjil Place Library, Melbourne 208, 209
Burapasarn, Bangkok 201

C

Café Central, Vienna 137
Café Fama, Weimar 152
Café Slavia, Prague 166
Café Tortoni, Buenos Aires 76
Caffe Trieste, San Francisco 46
Cairo **174–7**
Calle Donceles, Mexico City 60
Cannery Row, Monterey Bay 51
Cape Town 216
Capitol Hill Books, Washington, D.C. 33
Cartagena 214
Casa dos Bicos, Lisbon 127
Casa Rivas Mercado, Mexico City 61
Cecil Court, London 83
Central Library, Prague 165
Central Library, Seattle 40, 42
Central Library, Wellington 212
Centro Cultural Elena Garro, Mexico City 61
Cervantes Birthplace Museum, Madrid 123
Charles Dickens Museum, London 84
Cheongun Literature Library, Seoul 188
Chicago **26–9**
Chicklit, Vienna 136
City Library, Bangkok 200
City Lights, San Francisco 44, 46
Colette, Sidonie-Gabrielle 117
Concord 24–5
Confeitaria Colombo, Rio de Janeiro 73
Copenhagen **154–9**
Cuesta de Moyano, Madrid 118, 120

D

Daikanyama T-Site, Tokyo 196
Dante Alighieri 129, 133
Dasa Book Cafe, Bangkok 203
Daunt Books, London 80, 84

Delhi 217
Dickens, Charles 13, 20, 81, 83, 84, 95
Diwan Bookstore, Cairo 176
Douglass, Frederick 33
Drama Book Shop, The, New York City 14–15
Dubai 216
Dublin **106–9**
Duchess Anna Amalia Library, Weimar 150, 152
Dunedin 211, 217
Duolun Road Cultural Street, Shanghai 182
Durban 216
Dussmann, Berlin 145

E

Eagle and Child, The, Oxford 90
Eckermann Buchhandlung, Weimar 152
Edgar Allan Poe Cottage, New York City 16
Edinburgh **100–105**
El Ateneo Grand Splendid, Buenos Aires 74, 78
Elephant House, The, Edinburgh 104, *104*
El Fishawy Café, Cairo 174, 177
Elliott Bay Book Company, Seattle 42
El Péndulo, Mexico City 62–3
Emerson, Ralph Waldo 19, 20, 25
Empty Library, The, Berlin 142
Eterna Cadencia, Buenos Aires 77

F

Fabulosa Books, San Francisco 49
Faulkner House Books, New Orleans 37
Faulkner, William 35, 36, 37
Feira de Alfarrabistas, Lisbon 126
Florence **128–33**
Folger Shakespeare Library, Washington, D.C. 32
Forest Hills Cemetery, Boston 22
Franz Kafka Museum, Prague 166
Frederick Douglass National Historic Site, Washington, D.C. 33
Freud Museum, Vienna 136
Frugal Bookstore, Boston 21
Fundação Biblioteca Nacional, Rio de Janeiro 72
Fundación Borges, Buenos Aires 78

G

Galatoire's, New Orleans 36
García Márquez, Gabriel 60, 65, 66, 67, 68–9, 214
Garden District Book Shop, New Orleans 38
Gay on Wye, Hay-on-Wye 93
Gay's the Word, London 84
German National Library, Leipzig 146, 148
Giunti Odeon, Florence 130
Globe Bookstore & Café, Prague 165
Goethe, Johann Wolfgang von 147, 149, 151, 152, 153, 215
Goethehaus, Weimar 153
Grandes, Almudena 119, 122
GRAPHIC X DAISHIN, Seoul 186
Green Apple Books, San Francisco 47
Green Gables Heritage Place, Prince Edward Island 57
Gulp Fiction, Oxford 90

H

Hamlet's Kronborg 160–61
Hares & Hyenas, Melbourne 207
Harlem Renaissance, New York City **17**
Harold Washington Library Center, Chicago 28
Harvard Book Store, Boston 21
Haworth 98–9
Hawthorne, Nathaniel 19, 20, 25
Hay-on-Wye 92–3
Hemingway, Ernest 111, 112, 116, 119, 203
Historic Joy Kogawa House, Vancouver 55
Honesty Bookshop, Hay-on-Wye 93
Hotel Chelsea, New York City 16
Hotel Emblem, San Francisco 49
Hotel Monteleone, New Orleans 36
Hotel Sorrento, Seattle 43
Hughes, Langston 17, 31
Hugo, Victor 111, 116

I

Iona Abbey, Scotland 161
Isherwood, Christopher 141, 144
Istanbul **168–73**
Itaewon Books, Seoul 186

J

Jacob-und-Wilhelm-Grimm-Zentrum, Berlin 140, 142
Jakarta 217
Jane Austen Centre, The, Bath 96
Jimbocho Book Town, Tokyo 191, 195, 197
Joe and Rika Mansueto Library, The, Chicago 29
John Sandoe Books, London 82
John's Grill, San Francisco 48
Joyce, James 107, 108, 109

K

Kadıköy Sahafları, Istanbul 173
Kafka, Franz 135, 151, 163, 166, 167
Kamome Books, Tokyo 192
Karaköy, Istanbul 170
Karen Blixen's House, Rungstedlund 157
Katherine Mansfield House & Garden, Wellington 213
Keats House, London 86
Kilns, The, Oxford 91
Kitazawa Bookstore, Tokyo 194–5, 195
Klementinum, Prague 164
Kogawa, Joy 53, 55
Kolkata 217
Kramers, Washington, D.C. 32
Kronborg Castle, Denmark 160–61

L

La Closerie des Lilas, Paris 116

Lafayette Cemetery No. 1, New Orleans 38
La Pecera del Círculo de Bellas Artes, Madrid 123
Left Bank Books Collective, Seattle 43
Leipzig **146–9**
Ler Devagar, Lisbon 127
Les Deux Magots, Paris 115
L'Hôtel, Paris 115
Librairie Galignani, Paris 113
Librairie Jousseaume, Paris 116
Library Bar, Copenhagen 157
Library of Congress, Washington, D.C. 30, 31, 32
Librería de Ávila, Buenos Aires 76
Librería Desnivel, Madrid 120
Librería Miguel Miranda, Madrid 121
Librería San Ginés, Madrid 122
Librería Wilborada 1047, Bogotá 67
Lisbon **124–7**
Literary festivals 20, 39, 82, 97, 158, 208
see also Hay-on-Wye; Saint-Pierre-de-Clages
Livraria Bertrand, Lisbon 126
Livraria da Travessa, Rio de Janeiro 72
Livraria Folha Seca, Rio de Janeiro 73
London **80–87**, 161
London City, Buenos Aires 76
Los Angeles 214
Luxor Winter Palace Hotel 179
Lu Xun Park, Shanghai 182

M

Machado de Assis 71, 73
MacLeod's Books, Vancouver 54
Macondo Linear Park, Aracataca 69
Madrid **118–23**
Mahfouz, Naguib 175, 176, 177
Main Street, Haworth 99
Maison de Victor Hugo, Paris 116
Makar's Court, Edinburgh 100, 102
Mandarin Oriental, The, Bangkok 202
Manga Art Hotel, Tokyo 196
Mansfield, Katherine 211, 213
Marrakesh 216
Marsh's Library, Dublin 109
Massy Books, Vancouver 54
Matorral Librería, Bogotá 67
Mechanic's Institute Library, The, San Francisco 48
Melbourne **204–9**
Mexico City **58–63**
Milton H. Latter Memorial Library, New Orleans 39
Minoa Pera, Istanbul 171
Moda Pier Library, Istanbul 173
Montgomery, L M 56–7
Morgan Library and Museum, New York City 13
Morioka Shōten, Tokyo 196
Mr. B's Emporium of Reading Delights, Bath 96
Mumbai 216
Munro, Alice 53, 55
Murder and Mayhem, Hay-on-Wye 93
Museum of Innocence, Istanbul 170
Museum of Literature Ireland, Dublin 108
Museum of Modern Japanese Literature, Tokyo 195
Myopic Books, Chicago 29

N

Naguib Mahfouz Museum, Cairo 177
narrm ngarrgu Library, Melbourne 206
National Steinbeck Center, Salinas 51
Natsume Sōseki Memorial Museum, Tokyo 192
Neilson Hays Library, Bangkok 202
New Beacon Books, London 82
New Orleans **34–9**
New York City **10–17**

O

Old Absinthe House, The, New Orleans 36
Old Books, Bath 94, 96
Old Library, The, Dublin 106, 108
Old Manse, The, Concord 25
Old School Room, Haworth 99
Omni Parker House, Boston 20
Open Book, Tokyo 192
Open Books: A Poem Emporium, Seattle 42
Orchard House, Concord 24–5
Oscar Wilde House and Statue, Dublin 108
Österreichische Nationalbibliothek, Vienna 134, 136
Outdoor Library, Seoul 187
Oxford **88–91**

P

Paludan Book Café, Copenhagen 156
Pamuk, Orhan 169, 170
Paperback Bookshop, The, Melbourne 206
Paperback Exchange, Florence 131
Paris **110–17**
Passport Bookshop, Bangkok 200
Pegasus Books, Wellington 210, 212
Père Lachaise Cemetery, Paris 117
Persephone Books, Bath 97
Phil, Vienna 137
Philadelphia 214
Philological Library, Berlin 143
Piccola Farmacia Letteraria, Florence 132
Pilsen Community Books, Chicago 28
Poe, Edgar Allan 16, 214
Poetry Bookshop, The, Hay-on-Wye 93
Poetry Foundation, The, Chicago 26, 28
Poets House, New York City 12
Politics and Prose, Washington, D.C. 33
Portland 214
Porto 215
Prague **162–7**
Prince Edward Island 56–7
Pro qm, Berlin 144
Proust, Marcel 117, 215
Public Library, Boston 22–3
Public Library, Greater Cairo 177
Public Library, New York City 10, 13

Public Library, San Francisco 47
Public Library, Vancouver 52, 54

Q

Quebec 214
Quevedo Libros y Antigüedades, Bogotá 67

R

Readings Carlton, Melbourne 208
Real Gabinete Português de Leitura, Rio de Janeiro 70, 72
Residencia de Estudiantes, Madrid 123
Rialto Bridge, Venice 161
Rio de Janeiro **70–73**
Rome 215
Rotorbooks, Leipzig 148
Royal Danish Library, Copenhagen 154, 156, 156

S

Sahaflar Çarşısı, Istanbul 168, 170
Saint-Pierre-de-Clages 138–9
Salinas Valley 50–51
Salt Galata, Istanbul 171
San Francisco **44–9**, 50
Schillerhaus, Leipzig 148
Schiller Museum, Weimar 152
Scott Monument, Edinburgh 102
Seattle **40–43**
Seoul **184–9**
Shakespeare, William 32–3, 82–3, 160–61
Shakespeare and Company, Paris 110, 112
Shakespeare & Sons, Prague 165
Shakespeare's Globe, London 82–3
Shanghai **180–83**
Shanghai Library East 183
She Said, Berlin 145
Sinan Books Poetry Store, Shanghai 180, 183
Singapore 217
Songpa Book Museum, Seoul 187
Sooyeonsanbang, Seoul 188, 189
Spark, Muriel 101, 104
SS *Sudan* Nile Boat 179
Staatsbibliothek Potsdamer Straße, Berlin 143
Starfield Library, Seoul 184, 188
State Library of Victoria, Melbourne 204, 206
Stein, Gertrude 117
Steinbeck Country 50–51
Steinbeck, John 45, 50–51
St. George's, Berlin 145
Strahov Monastery Library, Prague 162, 164
Strand Bookstore, New York City 12
Sydney 217

T

Tama Cemetery, Tokyo 196
Tanpınar, Ahmet Hamdi 169, 170
Telegraphist's House, Aracataca 69
Te Matapihi ki te Ao Nui, Wellington 212
Temples of Abu Simbel 179
Thoreau, Henry David 19, 25
Tills Bookshop, Edinburgh 104, 105
Todo Modo, Florence 130
Tokyo **190–97**
Tolkien, J R R 89, 90, 91
Tongmungwan, Seoul 188
Topping & Company Booksellers, Bath 96
Topping & Company Booksellers, Edinburgh 103
Top Withens, Haworth 99
Toronto 214
Tower of London 161
Trinity College, Dublin 106, 108
Typewronger Books, Edinburgh 102

U

Ulysses Rare Books, Dublin 109
UNAM Central Library, Mexico City 62
Unity Books, Wellington 212
University Library, Copenhagen 158, 159
Upper Nile Valley, The 178–9
Upstart & Crow, Vancouver 54, 55

V

Vancouver **52–5**
Venice 161, 215
Vesuvio Cafe, San Francisco 46
Vienna **134–7**, 166
Villa Ocampo, Buenos Aires 78

W

Walking tours 17, 87, 117, 133, 167, 197
Waseda International House of Literature, Tokyo 193
Washington, D.C. **30–33**
Waterstones Piccadilly, London 83
Weimar **150–53**
Wellington **210–13**
White Horse Tavern, New York City 12
Wilde, Oscar 107, 108, 109, 115, 117
Willard Hotel, The, Washington, D.C. 32
Williams, Tennessee 35, 36, 39
Word on the Water, London 86
World at the Corner, Bangkok 201
Wright, Richard 27, 117
Writers' Museum, Edinburgh 102
Writers Walk, Wellington 213

Y

Ye Olde Cheshire Cheese, London 83

Z

Zikawei Library, Shanghai 182

Acknowledgments

DK would like to thank all the bookish folk who contributed to this book.

Editorial

Mark Baker is a longtime Prague resident, travel writer and author of *Čas proměn* ("Time of Changes"), a Czech-language account of the 1989 Velvet Revolution and its aftermath.

Jennifer Barger was a *Washington Post* fashion editor and a *National Geographic Travel* editor; her Substack, "The Souvenirist", explores the intersection of travel and retail.

Nicola Brady is a travel writer based in Dublin, who loves to rummage for well-thumbed travel guides in the city's bookshops.

Lucy Bryson is a British freelance travel writer and lifelong bookworm. She has spent two decades living in and writing about Brazil and Portugal, and loves reading on Rio's beaches.

Camila Daza is a Colombian writer who now lives in the UK and spends her spare time in bookish nooks, writing the hours away.

Lucie Grace is is a culture, travel and wellness writer in Thailand. A life-long book collector, her favorite authors are Deborah Levy and Muriel Spark.

Mary Gray is an American editor, writer, and journalist based in Italy. A longtime resident of Florence, she now has a room with a view in Turin.

Laura Hall is an author and travel journalist based in Copenhagen. She lives her life by one of Karen Blixen's mottoes: "The cure for everything is salt water: sweat, tears, or the sea."

Rebecca Hallett is a travel writer and Japan specialist, whose books include DK's *Ultimate Japan*. A favorite read is Masashi Matsuie's *Summer at Mount Asama*.

Rachel Laidler is a writer and editor for DK Travel and the author of *North Coast 500*. She loves nothing more than lingering in the Scottish capital's cozy bookshops.

Thom Lampon-Masters is a translator and Jean Rhys fanboy based in Madrid. He is currently slugging his way through a PhD in Latin American literature, his first novel-length translation, and the works of Proust.

Jessica Lee is a travel writer who specializes in North Africa and the Middle East. Find her browsing Diwan and the AUC Bookstore when in Cairo

Rachel Preece is a writer and editor living in Munich, though originally from the UK. She's a fan of German contemporary literature, and enjoys anything by Jenny Erpenbeck.

Alex Rennie landed in Berlin 12 years ago, wooed by the German capital's vibrant cultural scene (and nightclubs). Nowadays he can be found wandering Kreuzberg's bookstores.

Jacqueline Salomé is a Vancouver-based writer focused on social justice. She believes public libraries are the heart of communities, and she also counts Indigenous-owned Massy Books among her favourite city spots.

Lucy Sara-Kelly writes and edits travel books at DK, in London. Her work takes her (virtually) all around the world, but she much prefers to travel to *entirely* different worlds ... via her favorite fantasy novels.

Jennifer Fernández Solano was born and raised in Mexico City, where she grew up reading Carlos Fuentes and Gabo. She's spent hours sipping tea at El Péndulo in Polanco, absorbed in her latest read.

Kristen Shoates is a Nashville-based travel writer. She's fond of reading on the road and traveling in famous authors' footsteps (like Steinbeck's romps through Northern California).

Charles Usher lives in Milwaukee, Wisconsin, and writes about South Korea and the American Midwest. His favorite place to read is in one of Seoul's traditional *hanok* cafes.

Design

Martha Olivia is an illustrator based in England. She creates bold, immersive work inspired by nature, culture, and heritage. Each piece evolves through a thoughtful design process.

Marta Bescos is a Madrid-based photo editor who has contributed to countless DK travel books.

References for quotations

p11 column 1, line 11: Whitman, Walt (1860). *Leaves of Grass.* 3rd Edition. Boston: Thayer and Eldridge.
p12 column 2, line 1: Thomas, Dylan (1952). *In Country Sleep, and Other Poems.* 1st Edition. New York: New Directions.
p15 column 1, line 1: Shakespeare, William (1623). *As You Like It.*
p25 column 1, line 14: Thoreau, Henry David (1854). *Walden.* 1st Edition. Boston: Ticknor and Fields.

p27 column 1, lines 1–4: Mencken, Henry Louis (1920). *The Literary Capital of the United States.* London: *The Nation.*
p27 column 2, lines 4–5: Sandburg, Carl (1916). *Chicago Poems.* 1st Edition. New York: Henry Holt.
p32 column 1, lines 28–29: John Adams (1800). 6th Cong., 1st sess.
p32 column 2, line 28: King, Martin Luther, Jr. (1963).
p36 column 2, lines 3–4: Hemingway, Ernest (1940). *For Whom the Bell Tolls.* 1st Edition. New York: Charles Scribner's Sons.
p38 column 2, line 20: Twain, Mark (1883). *Life on the Mississippi.* 1st Edition. Boston: James R. Osgood.
p45 column 1, line 10: Steinbeck, John (1962). *Travels with Charley: In Search of America.* 1st Edition. New York: The Viking Press.
p51 column 1, lines 9–10: Steinbeck, John (1952). *East of Eden.* 1st Edition. New York: The Viking Press.
p57 column 1, line 5: Montgomery, Lucy Maud (1908). *Anne of Green Gables.* 1st Edition. Boston: L. C. Page & Company.
p69 column 1, lines 3–4: García Márquez, Gabriel (1996). *Gabo, El Otro, El Colombiano.*
p90 column 2, line 21: Merry in *The Lord of the Rings: The Fellowship of the Ring* (2001).
p91 column 2, line 10: Tolkien, J R R (1954). *The Fellowship of the Ring.* 1st Edition. London: George Allen & Unwin.
p99 column 1, line 9: Cathy in *Wuthering Heights* (1939).
p130 column 2, lines 1–3: de' Medici, Lorenzo (1490). *Canzona di Bacco (A Song for Bacchus).*
p133 column 3, lines 6–7: Alighieri, Dante (1308–1321). *The Divine Comedy.*
p161 column 2, line 17: Shakespeare, William (1623). *The Merchant of Venice.*
p179 column 1, line 1: Flaubert, Gustave (1981). *The Letters of Gustave Flaubert 1830–1857.* 1st Edition. London: Faber.
p192 column 2, lines 18–20: Soseki, Natsume (2010). *Kokoro.* London: Penguin Classics.
p222 column 1, lines 37–38: Dinesen, Isak. (1934). *Seven Gothic Tales.* 1st Edition. New York: Harrison Smith and Robert Haas.

Picture Credits

The publisher would like to thank the following for their kind permission to reproduce their photographs:

4Corners: Sandra Raccanello 149.
Adobe Stock: Dorota – stock.adobe.com 136; Geza Kurka – stock.adobe.com 16; Givaga 178–179, Stevan 64.
Alamy Stock Photo: AGENZIA SINTESI 126, Album 57, Album / The Christie Archive Trust. 179; Mark Andrews 182; Arcaid Images 29; ilyas Ayub 172; Andrew Baumert 142; BD Images 56–57; Jon Bilous 33; Gualtiero Boffi 192; Irina Brester 58; Ron Buskirk 40; CNMages 21, 116; Rodolfo Contreras 124; Danita Delimont Creative 30; Peter Delius 127; dpa picture alliance 132; FocusCulture 190; Tony French 80; Horst Friedrichs 86; Goddard Archive 93; Diego Grandi 79; Hemis / CHAREL Franck 177; Hemis / DOZIER Marc 70; Hemis / RIEGER Bertrand 166; ilpo musto 46; Image Professionals GmbH / Isabela Pacini 146; Imago 183; Imago / Wang Teng 202; InfotronTof 164; Brian Jannsen 24–25; Cristian Mihaila 160–161; Ben Molyneux 90; Thom Moore 104; William Morgan 39; Nikreates 38; Ahmet Selcuk Ozel 168; Kim Petersen 159; PulpFoto 91; Pulsar Imagens 72; ruelleruelle 203; scenicireland.com / Christopher Hill 106; Scherl / Süddeutsche Zeitung Photo 25; Alex Segre 83; SJArt 161; SMPNEWS 97; The Picture Art Collection 99; Ilias Trakadas 134; Wibowo Rusli 184.
Ambiente Familiar: Sebastián Cruz Roldán 67.
Nathalia Angarita: 68–69.
Cedric Angeles: 36, 37.
AWL Images: Jon Arnold 115, 137; Andrea Comi 65; Alan Copson 92–93; Hemis 114; Susanne Kremer 112; Jan Miracky 162; Nicholas Tinelli 74, 76, 77; Steve Vidler 85, 94.
Banco de la República: Alberto Sierra 66.
Solange Belon: 138–139, 139.
Biblioteca Nacional de España: Josefina Blanco 121.
Books & Company: 158.
Brattle Book Shop: 18.
Cafebrería El Péndulo: 62–63.
Chris da Canha: 186, 187, 189.
Confeitaria Colombo: Wagner Pinheiro 73.
CreatAR Images: 180.
Dreamstime.com: Byvalet 200; Pablo Meilan Campagnale 150; Filedimage 206; Vampy1 44.
Fabulosa Books: 49.
Getty Images: Corbis / Hulton Deutsch 51; Hulton Archive / Ulf Andersen 69; Moment / Martin Priestley 98–99; K.M. Westermann 174.
Getty Images / iStock: Pgiam 50–51; Takako Phillips 48; Oleh Slobodeniuk 198; Chunyip Wong 88.
Giunti Editore: 130.
Green Apple Books: 47.
Image Professionals GmbH: lookphotos 140.
Karen Blixen Museum Rungstedlund: Annemette Kuhlmann 157.
Katherine Mansfield House & Garden: Rob Suisted / www.naturespic.com 213.
Kitazawa Bookstore: 194–195.

Klassik Stiftung Weimar: Gordon Welters 153.
Matej Krén: 165.
Melbourne Athenaeum Library: Grace Petrou 207.
Robert Ormerod: 100, 102, 103, 105.
Pegasus Books: 210, 212.
Sandra Pereznieto: 61.
Pike Place Market PDA: 43.
Pro qm Bookshop: KM Dietrich 144.
James Rajotte: 9, 118, 120, 122, 123.
Readings Carlton: 208.
Reuters: Mohamed Abd El Ghany 176.
Shakespeare and Company: Hugo Clair Torregrosa 6, 110.
She Said: Savannah van der Niet 145.
Shutterstock.com: Acropolypse Photography 171; Alex Cimbal 209; DameTraveler 113; DW labs Incorporated 12; Chayanit Itthipongmaetee 60; marcobriviophotographer 13; Resul Muslu 173.
Stabi Berlin: nilo – Agentur für Fotografie 143.
Robert Stefanowicz: 52.
The British Institute of Florence: 131.
The Drama Book Shop: 14–15.
The Poetry Foundation: MELLADRAMATIC 26.
The Shakespeare Globe Trust: Leora Bermeister, Farelight Productions 62.
Kisa Toyoshima: 193.
Ulysses Rare Books: Ken Walsh 109.
University of Copenhagen, Copenhagen University Library Fiolstræde: Laura Stamer 154, 156.
Unsplash: Daniel Brubaker 22–23; NIR HIMI 204; Rosie Kerr 34; Pixel Parker 10.
Upstart & Crow: 55.
World at the Corner: 201.

DK Penguin Random House

Project Editor Lucy Sara-Kelly
Senior Editor Lucy Richards
Senior Designer Michael Curia
Editors Catrina Conway, Rachel Laidler, Eleanora Reeves
Senior US Editor Megan Douglass
Proofreader Clare Diston
Indexer Elizabeth Wise
Picture Researcher Marta Bescos
Senior Cartographic Editor Suresh Kumar
Jacket and Sales Material Coordinator Serena Sclocco
Illustrator and Jacket Designer Martha Olivia
Image Retoucher Michelle Briers
Senior Production Editor Tony Phipps
Senior Production Controller Kariss Ainsworth
Managing Art Editor Michael Duffy
Editorial Director Hollie Teague
Art Director Maxine Pedliham
Publishing Director Georgina Dee

First American Edition 2026
Published in the United States by DK Publishing
a division of Penguin Random House LLC
1745 Broadway, 20th Floor, New York, NY 10019

Copyright © 2026 Dorling Kindersley Limited
26 27 28 29 30 10 9 8 7 6 5 4 3 2 1
001–362671–Sep/2026

All rights reserved.
Without limiting the rights under the copyright reserved above, no part of this publication may be reproduced, stored in or introduced into a retrieval system, or transmitted, in any form, or by any means (electronic, mechanical, photocopying, recording, or otherwise), without the prior written permission of the copyright owner.

DK values and supports copyright. Thank you for respecting intellectual property laws by not reproducing, scanning or distributing any part of this publication by any means without permission. By purchasing an authorized edition, you are supporting writers and artists and enabling DK to continue to publish books that inform and inspire readers.

No part of this publication may be used or reproduced in any manner for the purpose of training artificial intelligence technologies or systems. In accordance with Article 4(3) of the DSM Directive 2019/790, DK expressly reserves this work from the text and data mining exception.
Published in Great Britain by Dorling Kindersley Limited

ISBN: 979-8-2173-1080-7

Printed and bound in China

www.dk.com

FSC www.fsc.org MIX Paper FSC™ C018179